WHAT OTHERS SAY

"Good writers use words to communicate ideas rather than to impress their readers. Michael Helms is a good writer who takes us on soft childhood memory trips or into the hard issues of current news with a mature, inquiring faith as his lens. Michael has expanded his pastoral ministry by discovering the secret of writing simply, yet intelligently."

John D. Pierce, Executive Editor,
Baptists Today, Macon, Georgia

Michael Helms provides an honest and compassionate look at life's journey in all of its complexities and unexpected outcomes—both good and bad. He prods and encourages us to embrace our struggles with humility, good humor, and with the reassurance that we are not alone. Michael shows us there are lessons for us to learn along the way and more than enough hope and mercy to help us become what we are meant to be.

Michael Braswell, Ph.D., Professor,
East Tennessee State University.

"Indeed, each of us begins each day finding our way. For some, the struggle is much greater than for others. For some the path may seem clear, and for some there is much fog covering that road. As Christians we plow through many Scriptures looking for answers, only to find that some issues will always be cloaked in mystery, and therefore we must rely on our faith to compensate for those times when we lack in understanding. And in all of this, applying lessons and testament put in print thousands of years ago remains an incredible challenge: what does this mean to me, today? That's the prevailing question for many of us. In *Finding Our Way*, the Rev. Michael Helms offers great insight in the application of centuries-old Biblical wisdom in a time of rocket ships and cyberspace. These nuggets of spiritual experience and exploration provide inspiration and enlightenment, helping us along the course of finding our way."

Dwain Walden, Editor and Publisher,
The Moultrie Observer, Moultrie, Georgia

"There is a natural affinity between the gospel and good stories. Like Jesus' parables, Helms' stories often draw from rural life, recall experiences we can all relate to, and then stay with us long after we read them. They heighten our appreciation for truth in the midst of the ordinary. Read the book for the stories. You will take away not only the stories but a deeper appreciation for the struggles, the small pleasures, and the God-given goodness of life also."

R. Alan Culpepper, Dean,
McAfee School of Theology, Atlanta, Georgia

finding our way

AN INTROSPECTIVE JOURNEY THROUGH THE LABYRINTH OF LIFE

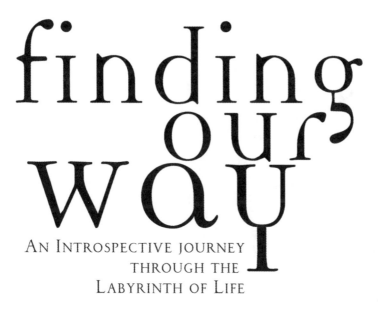

finding our way

An Introspective journey through the Labyrinth of Life

john michael helms

WINEPRESS WP PUBLISHING

ISBN 1-57921-833-4
Library of Congress Catalog Card Number: 2005905287

Dedication

To Wassie Vickery, who first
encouraged me to write

To Dwain Walden, who gave me
my first opportunity to write for the public

To Andrea Savage, who continues
to make me a better writer

To Trinity Baptist Church,
who allow me the opportunity
to pastor, to preach, to write,
and to join them in finding our way
through the labyrinth of life

table of contents

introduction

The complex system of chambers and passageways of the inner ear is called a labyrinth. Both the hearing and balance portions of the inner ear are included in this system of chambers and passageways. When sound travels unhindered through these narrow chambers and passageways, we recognize the sounds and we maintain a sense of balance necessary for mobility.

The word "labyrinth" is derived from the Greek word for maze. Like the maze of hedges of the front cover of this book, life is filled with many choices as we find our way, some of which can get us lost or lead to dead ends. Through the centuries, both philosophers and theologians have sought to answer questions about a life that has its share of maze-like qualities. We can become frustrated and even give up. With so much room for error, when we find our way, the joy is magnified.

Wouldn't it be great if we had someone to start us at the beginning of the journey, point us in the correct direction, and tell us all we have to do is follow the path and it will lead us directly to the center, to a place of peace, a place of contentment? Once we get to the center, all we have to do is begin the journey again and we will find our way back home. If we stay on the path, we can't get lost. I have just described to you how a labyrinth works.

A labyrinth is a circular pattern featuring a serpentine but clear path to the center. Labyrinths have been around for more than a thousand years. They were set as mosaics into the floors of Gothic cathedrals. Pilgrims, both past and present, have walked labyrinths to the center and back out again in a kind of walking meditation, seeking answers and direction, peace and contentment.

The first time I saw a labyrinth was during a study trip to Saskatchewan, Canada. The retreat center had a beautiful A-framed chapel, glassed at both ends, which let in the dazzling light of the sun and gave a beautiful view of the woods behind the chapel.

Peering through the glassed end of the chapel, I noticed a strange grassed maze at the bottom of the hill. It looked like one of those mazes you find in children's magazines, which invite children to enter the maze, pencil in hand, and draw their way out the other end. Upon a closer look, I discovered my very first labyrinth.

There I saw people walking in a labyrinth for the first time. Before entering the circle, some people took off their shoes. They walked slowly around the circle, stopping at various places, praying, meditating, and holding out their hands as if God might drop some blessing from heaven for them to catch.

I'd like for you to use this book in this way—like a labyrinth. It's a book designed to assist you on your current journey. I have no idea what journey you are on or where you are in your journey. The beauty of a labyrinth is that the details don't matter as much as the intentional soul searching we all need to do as we find our way in this world.

Somewhere within the chapters of this book, you will find something that helps you in your journey. The chapters are designed to take you deeper and deeper into the labyrinth until you reach the center. There you will explore what I believe belongs at the center of all our journeys: facing our finiteness, our mortality. Until we have come to terms with the fact that we are dust and to dust we shall return, we are not prepared to make a return journey out of the labyrinth and into a world where we are not only free, but compelled to offer our lives as living sacrifices to the God who made us and to the God who has the power and desire to redeem us and to set us free for a life of service.

Since it is impossible for us to journey apart from our own story or apart from being a part of the stories of other people, each chapter begins with a story. You are encouraged to find how each story intersects with your own or how your story differs from the one that is told. Find a character with whom you most identify and feel the emotion that character brings to the story.

I will use each story as a launching pad to discuss issues raised by the story. Two of the chapters contain an additional story for added reflection. At the end of each chapter, questions will be asked and meditative thoughts will be raised to help you address issues in your own journey. The goal for each chapter is to provide reflective material that will be of use to you as you find your way through this part of your life.

With the Holy Spirit as your guide, enter this book as you would a labyrinth, with a desire to follow the path, being open to where the path will carry you. Listen as the Lord speaks to you through the stories at the beginnings of these chapters and through the essays which follow. Wade into the questions and the directive statements at the ends of the chapters.

If used as a serious form of self-reflection, these stories, essays, and questions can assist you on your current journey. If the chambers and passageways of your spiritual life have become clogged, resulting in the loss of some of your spiritual hearing, this book will help you hear the Lord's voice afresh. If you have developed spiritual vertigo, a journey through these stories and essays may help you regain your balance and find your way to the center of the Lord's will.

Even if your walk with the Lord is strong, walking through this labyrinth of stories, essays, reflective questions, and directed exercises will make your journey even stronger and can help you assist others who may be struggling to find their way.

We are fellow companions on a common journey. Enter now this book with me and let's find our way on this introspective journey through the labyrinth of life.

CHAPTER ONE

soaring High and crashing Down

Illustration by Tina Piemonte

THE BIRD DOG

My soul clings to you; your right hand upholds me.

—Psalm 63:8

A little boy sat by the ocean and watched the birds surf the wind. As he observed the birds soar overhead, an idea came to him. *I'll build my own bird,* he thought. He took some sticks, paper, and tape and fashioned a bird straight from his imagination. With the excitement that the Wright brothers must have felt at Kitty Hawk, he pushed the stick and paper bird through the air hoping to set it free to soar with the other birds. But the invisible forces of the earth pulled his creation down time and time again.

As hard as he tried, the little boy decided his bird could never soar like a real one. With imagination still working, he simply decided to call his creation a dog instead. He tied a string to the paper and stick dog and pulled it along the beach. "Come on, boy," he yelled as he began to run, paper dog in tow. As the boy ran faster and faster, the wind created enough lift that the boy's stick and paper creation rose above the beach and waves.

Friends walked by and complimented the boy on his creation. "What is it?" some asked curiously. "It's a bird dog," the boy replied with a smile, struggling to keep his creation in the air as it moved sharply in one direction and then another.

"Shouldn't a dog have a tail?" asked a little girl who stood watching. From her hair she pulled two ribbons and tied them together. "Here's your dog a tail," she said. He pulled in his creation and tied the tail onto his bird dog.

Once again the boy ran with the bird dog, and it lifted into the sky, higher and higher. The tail gave the bird dog the stability it needed to remain calm in the swift currents of wind. The boy watched proudly as it flew with the ocean birds. He felt it was something of a miracle that his creation of sticks, paper, and tape had taken a life of its own.

He bragged about his creation to those who came by. He began to tell people his bird dog could fly as well as any ocean bird. One beach walker reminded the boy that the bird dog could fly only because of the tension on the string. "Don't let go of that string," came the advice, "or your bird dog will come crashing down."

Though he held it in his right hand, the boy had forgotten about the string. It should have been obvious to him that it was what made the difference between his bird dog and the ocean birds that circled overhead. However, by now the boy was convinced that his creation had really learned to fly and the string was no longer needed.

Instead of listening to the advice of the beach walker, the boy let go of the string. At first the bird dog went higher and higher and farther and farther away. "It's flying, it's flying!" yelled the boy. But then he noticed it was sinking from the sky, faster and faster. Far out into the ocean, the bird dog crashed.

The next morning the boy walked out on the beach. With the ocean birds circling overhead, he sat to ponder the fate of his creation. As he sat and watched the waves beat against the shore, he noticed the tide had deposited the remains of the bird dog on the beach during the night. He ran over to examine the remains. Everything was ruined. The paper, the tape, the sticks could not be used again. Then he noticed the string.

He remembered the tension he had felt in his hands as the bird dog rode the shifting currents of the wind. He had let go of the string because he felt that the tension was keeping his creation from being like all the other ocean birds. But now he realized the beach walker was right. The string and the tension it created between his hands and his bird dog gave it the freedom to fly. The boy rolled up the wet string and placed it in his pocket. It was worth saving for his next creation. Next time, he would be sure not to let go.

INTENTIONAL JOURNEYS BEGIN WITH DREAMERS

With few exceptions, everyone has sat dreaming with this little boy. The nature of our dreams and the content of our dreams are unique to our own time and place, but dreaming is one of the common denominators of the human race, transcending race, sex, and culture.

Our dreams can be holy or profane, well-guided or misplaced, realistic or impossible. Our dreams may act as catapults, thrusting us into goal-making, action-planning enthusiasts, intent on making our dreams come true at all costs. For the underprivileged, the unmotivated, or those unwilling to take risks, dreams may serve only as a temporary respite from an otherwise difficult situation or mundane life—a type of day-dreaming that fills a gap of time without ever being considered as possible enough to try.

New journeys begin with dreams. Those who don't dream still journey, but they are like a leaf that falls into a stream. They are captive to the currents, the crevices of the rocks, and the churning of the water. They have no ability to alter their course. They are moving, but they are moving to a destination that is not of their choosing.

Dreamers are more like kayakers who see possibilities in the currents. Instead of being at the mercy of the rapids, these adventurous souls dream of new and creative ways to attack the rapids. With special moves called enders, pirouettes, whippets, and McTwists, these imaginative people add new meaning to the word "journey." With every successful run, confidence builds, spawning the dreaming of new possibilities.

SOME SETTLE FOR SECOND BEST

Not all dreamers succeed. That is a good thing. What if Hitler had succeeded in his dream to rule the world? It's a good thing that not everything we dream about comes true, either. Not all our dreams are holy. Many of them aren't even close. They are often self-centered, self-serving, and self-indulging.

We also have worthy dreams that don't succeed. These failures must be carefully evaluated, so we can learn from our mistakes.

In the story of the boy and the kite, there is nothing wrong with the boy's dream to build a bird that could soar like the birds of the sea. For a child, it was an extremely ambitious and admirable dream, but as soon as his dream came crashing down, he was content to call his creation a dog, and he soon forgot about his lofty dream.

"He just became more realistic," you might say. Perhaps. I say he gave up on his dream too quickly. If we give up on worthy dreams too quickly, we end up settling for second best and we forfeit the joy realized dreams would have brought as well as new possibilities.

Far too many people quit dreaming after the first failure in life. They run along the beach of life pulling lost hopes and trying to put on a happy face, hoping others will believe they are content when in reality they are miserable. It's sad when a person goes through life pulling one lost dream after another, never finding meaning or purpose. We can discover the meaning and purpose for our lives only when the mystical wind of God's Holy Spirit blows in our lives and gently pushes us in a holy direction.

THE SPIRIT OF GOD CREATES NEW POSSIBILITIES

Jesus told Nicodemus that the wind (Spirit) blows where it wishes. You can hear the sound of it, but you cannot tell where it comes from or where it goes. "So it is," Jesus said, of "everyone who is born of the Spirit" (John 3:8).

For those who are seeking to journey on a path of faith, this is good news. It means that finding our way is not dependent upon our dreaming alone. God, the first dreamer of all creation, chooses His own time and way for His Spirit to blow in our lives. The Lord is the wind. We are the sails. The Lord is the captain. We are the first mate. The Lord is the rudder. We are the vessel. The Lord is the thrower. We are the dream catchers.

The Spirit blows where it wishes and creates new possibilities in our lives. If we are smart, we will run with the opportunity created by God's Spirit. We will hold onto our faith, and the Lord will cause our hopes to rise and to soar as we discover that God has allowed our dreams to be fulfilled. We may also discover new possibilities we did not know would be ours.

Jesus once said,

> Most assuredly, I say to you, he who believes in Me, the works that I do he will do also; and greater works than these he will do, because I go to My Father. 13 And whatever you ask in My name, that I will do, that the Father may be glorified in the Son. 14 If you ask anything in My name, I will do it.
>
> —John 14:12-14 NKJV

19

There's no greater feeling in the world than to experience the wind of the Spirit of God lift up our lives. Yet, ironically, the moment we begin to soar may become our biggest test of all.

PRIDE GOES BEFORE A FALL

Once the boy's bird began to fly, he began to get attention. Attention is a double-edged sword. On the positive side of the blade is the self-esteem it builds, a much-needed part of building character. On the negative side of the blade is that the attention received from our gifts and abilities can cause us to trust in ourselves and not in the God who blessed us with our gifts and abilities.

Hubris is the root of original sin. In the first story of humankind in the Bible, the storyteller shares that the entire garden was a gift to both man and woman. Only two things were kept from them, the Tree of Knowledge of Good and Evil and the Tree of Life. God gave them the freedom to enjoy all the amenities of the garden but forbade them to eat the fruit of these trees.

The serpent's genius was his knowledge of the weak area of human nature—our desire to be our own gods. The serpent convinced the woman that she knew enough to make decisions apart from God. Any time we substitute our judgment for the judgment of God, the original sin plays out in our lives all over again. Incidentally, "I" is in the middle of pride just as it is in the middle of sin.

At first the boy with the kite accepted that he didn't have all he needed, and the gift of the girl's ribbon helped steady his kite. But then as others came by to look at his creation floating in the sky, he began to believe his kite would do well even without the tension on the string. When the boy let go of the string, he enjoyed a moment of exhilaration, followed by the grief of losing what he had worked for.

This reminds me of a scene from a Charlie Brown and Lucy cartoon. As Charlie Brown follows the string to his downed kite, he says to his friend and nemesis, Lucy: "In kite-flying the ratio of weight to sail-area is very important. This ratio is known as 'Sail Loading' and it is measured in ounces per square foot. For example, a three-foot kite with a sail area of four and one-half square feet should weigh about two or three ounces." Lucy observes, "You know a lot about kites, don't you, Charlie Brown?" He replies, "Yes, I think I can say that I do." By this time the string has led them to the mouth of a storm drain—where the string disappears. In the last frame Lucy asks, "Then why is your kite down the sewer?"[1]

How does the Bible put it? "Pride goes before destruction, and a haughty spirit before a fall" (Proverbs 16:18 NKJV).

MANY JOURNEYS ARE LITTERED WITH BROKENNESS

Most of the time, we don't have to be told our kite has crashed. Of course there are those who live in denial that their lives have unraveled. Sadly, some people never acknowledge life has crashed around them. They refuse to change or acknowledge that their lives are in pieces.

There are others, though, who understand and acknowledge the feelings of loss the boy felt as he found the remains of his kite washed up on the beach. Life is lined with the fabric of loss and brokenness. These cannot be avoided completely. When loss is due to our lack of obedience to heed God's direction and even when loss comes due to no fault of our own, there are great lessons to be learned. In the first case, the key to finding our way is to acknowledge we have sinned and fallen short of God's glory. We must then look to Jesus to restore us in the Lord's favor. In the second case, where great loss comes due to no fault of our own, such as happened to Job, the key to finding our way is to hold onto the cord of faith, even though we do not understand the world or the events that have transpired within it.

Faith is much easier when we can find a reason for our brokenness. We are people who live in a world of cause and effect. As scientific-minded people, we look for a reason for every action. We are not comfortable living with ambiguity or mystery. When there does not seem to be any apparent reason for evil, suffering, or hardship, maintaining our faith can become a struggle.

Job said, "Though He slay me, yet will I trust Him" (Job 13:15 NKJV). Why trust a God who does not always protect us from the injustices of life?

This was a question the Psalmist had to ask when he looked around and saw the prosperity of the wicked while it seemed that only ills plagued him even though he sought to keep his heart pure.

> When I tried to understand all this, it was oppressive to me till I entered the sanctuary of God; then I understood their final destiny. Surely you place them on slippery ground; you cast them down to ruin. How suddenly are they destroyed, completely swept away by terrors! As a dream when one awakes, so when you arise, O Lord, you will despise them as fantasies.
> —Psalm 73:16-20

For the Psalmist, the key to finding his way was to hold onto his faith and trust that God would eventually, in His timing, work out issues of justice. Though he didn't have all the answers, the Psalmist continued to believe in a God who did. He had to learn to be content with worshiping a God who does not always reveal His ways to us.

The Psalmist reminds us that the key to finding our way is to acknowledge that God is always with us, holding us by His right hand, guiding us with his counsel, and will one day fully redeem us in heaven (Psalm 73:23-24).

"Whom have I in heaven but you?" asks the Psalmist. "Earth has nothing I desire besides you. My flesh and my heart may fail, but God is the strength of my heart and my portion forever" (Psalm 73:25-26).

GOD IS STILL IN THE BUSINESS OF REDEEMING

As the boy sat by the ocean, he observed what parts of his kite were ruined and what parts were salvageable. He rolled up the string, remembering it was the tension on the string that was the key in keeping his kite in the air.

It is this tension, our faith in God, that keeps our spirit elevated and helps us maintain a healthy perspective on what part God plays and what part we play as we journey together. Life takes many unexpected turns, sometimes causing people to let go of their faith. Pride can push faith out of a person's life. Tragedy and suffering have caused other people to let go of their faith. Still others have let go of their faith because God did not answer a prayer as they desired.

At the beginning of the seventy-third Psalm the Psalmist admitted he almost lost the foothold on his faith. Doubt had crept into his mind, and he wondered if God saw or cared about his condition. "My steps had nearly slipped. For I was envious of the boastful, When I saw the prosperity of the wicked" (Psalm 73:2-3 NKJV).

The Psalmist resolved his issues by entering into the sanctuary of God. He doesn't say what motivated him to go. He just went. While seeking God in the context of worship, the Psalmist began to feel the tension of faith coming back into his life.

Worship and attending church are not synonymous. Most people have attended church at one time or another without having a worshipful experience. All Christians should realize that worship involves our total self, and thus, we can worship God at any time and in any place. Even so, there is a lot of power in worshiping God with other believers. We are more likely to find our way when we make the intentional effort of walking into the sanctuary of God with the purpose of hearing his voice and finding our own among a chorus of other believers or seekers intent on finding the Lord.

In China, 2600 years before the birth of Christ, a great general by the name of Genghis Khan made a name for himself. Under his leadership, his men defeated enemy after enemy. Genghis had one problem, though. After wandering so far from home to defeat neighboring armies, he had trouble finding his way home. What could be more embarrassing for a great man of war than to get his men lost while returning from war?

Genghis was fortunate enough to have some intelligent men in his army who helped him solve his problem. Imagine the good humor that may have occurred one day as horses rode into the camp pulling a chariot with a wooden man standing tall with an arm pointed in a fixed direction. "Sir, we have a gift for you. Now after we have defeated our enemies we can rely on this wooden man to point us in the direction of our homes." At first it may have appeared to be a joke. Then the genius of the men unfolded as the geared mechanisms of the chariot were explained. The complex gears worked together in such a way that regardless of which direction the horses went or how many times they turned the chariot, the wooden soldier that stood on top always pointed in the direction of home.

A miniature replica of this chariot, known as a "South-Pointing Chariot," is on exhibit at the Smithsonian Institution in Washington, D.C. Several years ago, an elderly friend of mine, Robert Adair, showed me the replica he built for his students at Moultrie Technical College. At first glance, the geared chariot looks like a child's toy. Upon close examination, it becomes obvious that, even with a set of plans, such a device takes a bit of genius to build.

Robert researched this project, developed his own set of plans, and built a "South-Pointing Chariot" as a model to challenge the advanced students in his shop class. Thinking about the "South-Pointing Chariot," Robert once wrote: "Do you think it would be a good idea to give all our church members one of these so they can find their way back to the church next Sunday after they leave?"

That's a great idea because so many people seem to lose their way. Somewhere along the way people forget what the tug of faith feels like. That often happens when people cease expressing their faith in the context of congregational worship. It also happens when people believe they can soar on their own, so they let go of their connection with a body of faithful believers.

Have you lost your way? Do you need to be reoriented in the direction of God's house? The habit of worship will not alleviate all doubt. Nor will all our faith questions be answered. Nevertheless, the Bible clearly points us back to the body of believers. "Let us not give up meeting together, as some are in the habit of doing, but let us encourage one another and all the more as you see the Day approaching" (Hebrews 10:25).

God is still in the business of redemption. He's used to saving a remnant in order to begin anew. The boy with the kite saved a remnant. He kept the string to use with his next creation. The string reminded him of the success he once had, a success created by wind and the tension on the line.

If you have lost your way, perhaps you can recall a time when the Spirit of God blew fresh winds in your life. Remember how you held on to God? Remember how you began to rise to new heights? Perhaps it's time to enter the sanctuary again. Perhaps it's time to let God do his work of redeeming you and helping you find your way. Trying to do it on our own is pride. And you know what's in the middle of pride, don't you?

Original drawing by Robert Ferré. Final graphic by Vicki Keiser.

Walking the Labyrinth

1. Imagination can release imprisoned possibilities. When you are imaginative and creative, what are you doing? Who are you with? What feelings do you have? Does your imagination carry you closer to or farther away from God?

2. Strong winds will blow us off course in life. Maintaining stability requires hard work and the grace of God. If your life is stable, even though strong currents have blown, thank God and identify what you are doing that's helping you maintain your course. If you are in danger of crashing and need a stabilizer, think of three changes you can make right now that will stop your erratic pattern and help you rise above the waves.

3. As we find our way, success can lead to arrogance. We can be like the rooster that thought the sun rose to hear him crow. Arrogance fills us up with ourselves and leaves little room for God. In what areas of life have you allowed arrogance

to push God out? Where do you need to decrease so God might increase?

4. Warning! Along the way we may be tempted to let go of our faith. This can happen in good times or in bad times. Read how the Psalmist resolved his faith crises and continued on his journey of faith.

5. Where is the tug of faith in your life the strongest? Where is it the weakest? What do you need to do to maintain a positive tug of faith between you and God? What faith disciplines have you laid down that you need to pick back up?

6. Life has many broken moments. Thankfully, we don't have a Humpty Dumpty God. God is in the business of putting us back together. God saves remnants in our lives that become part of our healing process: memories, feelings, Scripture passages, promises, friends, special moments, and conversations, to name a few. What good thing are you holding on to that God might use to begin your healing process?

CHAPTER TWO

caring for yourself
along the way

THE CANOPY ROAD EXPERIENCE

Pastor Baker checked with his secretary to find out who was hospitalized. She reminded him that Mrs. Carter was still in ICU in Tallahassee, Florida, a seventy-mile drive from Pastor Baker's home in Moultrie, Georgia.

Finding your way from Moultrie to Tallahassee is simple. Highway 319 South will carry you through Thomasville, past a few old Southern plantations, through the area DeSoto explored in the 1500's, and into Northern Tallahassee, an area teeming with new residential and business growth.

Pastor Baker worked out his schedule and informed his secretary of his itinerary. "Do you always travel 319 South to get to Tallahassee?" asked his secretary. "Well, I didn't know there was another way," Pastor Baker responded. "There is another way," his secretary replied. "It adds a little more time to the trip but it's well worth it."

"Time is something I have precious little of," responded Pastor Baker. "If it's a longer trip, I'll just go the way I've always gone."

His secretary knew that her boss often found it easier to care for others than for himself. She knew getting him to try this alternate route would require a little trickery.

"I understand you are short of time, but I really need you to do me a favor. I have a letter I need to get to the owner of Bradley's store. If you take the alternative route I'll show you, you'll go right by the store. It'll only add about ten minutes to your trip."

"I don't mind doing that at all," Pastor Baker responded. Little did he know he'd just been tricked into doing something for himself.

The secretary scribbled a few words on a piece of paper which she put in a sealed envelope along with a few dollars. On the outside of the envelope she wrote: "To the Owner of Bradley's Store." She gave it along with directions to the pastor, and he was off into his busy day.

Once he got to Thomasville, he pulled out his secretary's directions.

Directions to Bradford's Store: Travel 319 South through Thomasville and turn left on Highway 122. This road takes you through the logging community of Metcalf. Highway 122 becomes Highway 59 after you cross the Florida line. Turn right at Miccosukee onto Highway 151 (Moccasin Gap Road). Moccasin Gap Road is a canopy road. Bradley's store is about ten miles down the road on the left. Enjoy!

"Enjoy?" Pastor Baker was in his usual rushed pace. He usually didn't think much about enjoying his drives. But once he turned onto Miccosukee Gap Road, he noticed how the gnarled oak branches snaked their way across the road forming a shaded canopy. The sun struggled to find a place to shoot a beam through the trees, occasionally sneaking in a ray here and there to reflect off the windshield of his car. Spanish moss hung from the trees that seemed to wave at him as he went by. He began to see them as his friends during his brief journey. They were like soldiers guarding the road, refusing to let through big noisy trucks or any other vehicle that might destroy the serenity of the environment. Their branches acted like crossed swords held out before him. He moved through them feeling like an honored guest.

The speed limit on the road was forty-five miles per hour. Normally such slow speeds frustrated a man who ran from appointment to appointment nonstop. But on this trip, he actually found himself enjoying the slow pace, realizing that to go any faster would cause him to miss much of the beautiful scenery.

The drive reminded him of days when he rode in slow cars with his grandparents, people who seemed to have all day to get where they were going. Perhaps that was why he liked driving his 1965 Comet, a car he had purchased from his grandmother and had restored. Whenever he got behind the wheel of that car he didn't feel rushed. He actually gave himself permission to slow down. He felt to do otherwise would be disrespectful to his grandmother who never drove the car more than fifty-five miles per hour.

Halfway between Miccosukee and Tallahassee, Pastor Baker came to Bradley's Country Store, which looks much as it did when it was built in 1927. His secretary knew her boss was a nostalgic man at heart. She had no doubt the setting of this store would appeal to him.

He stopped the car and walked up onto the wooden porch of the store. As he opened the screened door, he thought he'd stepped back in time. His eyes were immediately drawn to the slick hardwood floors, smoothed by generations of shuffling feet of customers looking for some dry goods or a bit of meat. Home-baked cookies filled old Tom's candy jars, which sat on the counter next to the register.

There was no one at the register. "Anybody here?" asked the pastor in a raised voice. The man running the store was in the back cutting some meat and a piece of cheese for a customer. "Be with you in just a moment, sir," came the reply.

Pastor Baker walked to the back of the store and waited until the man finished with the customer. "My secretary asked that I deliver this to you," he said. "Well, what is it?" "I don't know. She didn't say. I was headed to Tallahassee to the hospital, and she just asked me if I'd come a different way and deliver this to you." "Well, thank you," said the store owner as he opened the envelope curiously.

31

Pastor Baker turned to leave. He was almost to the door when the store owner hollered, "Sir, would you have a seat in the rocker on the porch for just a minute? When I finish with this customer, I need to speak to you."

Pastor Baker was a bit impatient with another delay in his schedule. Nevertheless, he couldn't help admitting that the scenery of the horses grazing across the road made the wait very pleasant. The customer left the store, and, after a few minutes, the store owner came out with a slice of sharp cheddar cheese inside a homemade biscuit in one hand and an eight-ounce Coke in the other. "Compliments of your secretary," he said. "It comes with these instructions." He handed the pastor a small piece of paper containing these words from his secretary: "As you find your way today, don't forget to slow down enough to appreciate God's world along with a mid-morning snack. Remember, it's OK to take a little time for yourself to reflect and to pray."

Pastor Baker smiled. As he rocked in the chair, it had already occurred to him that he was as relaxed as a dog sleeping in the sun on a cold day. The canopy road and the old country store had caused him to shift gears, and he wasn't denying that it felt good.

Driving down Moccasin Gap Road and sitting at Bradley's Country Store made him wonder what life would be like if he actually lived along a canopy road. Would he slow down? Would he have the same appreciation for its beauty? Would he find relaxing moments to reflect? Or would the trees become commonplace? Would he curse the speed limit and wish the lady ahead of him would speed up so he could get to his meeting on time? Would he slow down or just move at the same fast pace he was used to?

Pastor Baker finished his cheese biscuit and downed the last swallow of Coke. *Why is it that Coke tastes better in an eight-ounce bottle?* he wondered. He made his way to the car less hurried than he'd gotten out. As he continued to find his way to Tallahassee, his mind turned to the sermon his secretary had preached to him, and one he'd likely preach in the near future.

It's important to be intentional and turn off the main road, away from the traffic, through the serenity of the woods in order to get lost for a while in our thoughts and in our conversation with God. The refreshment of the journey will help prepare us for a more hurried pace when we return to the hurry-scurry world to which we have become so accustomed. We need to turn off the main roads more often and enjoy the canopy road experience. When that's not possible, we need to find ways to turn the commonplace roads we normally travel into canopy road experiences. For when we learn to care for ourselves, we have more energy to care for others, not less.

It's OK to Care for Ourselves

The pastor in this story is representative of all those people in caring professions and caring roles who find it difficult to care for themselves. Many people feel guilty when they set aside their responsibilities for others long enough to travel down a canopy road. Rather than feel guilty, many simply choose not to care for themselves properly. We pay a price for our choices. The price we pay can be the loss of our own emotional and physical health and breakdowns in relationships with others we love. I've known people who literally ran away from it all because they didn't know how else to handle the stress.

Such feelings were expressed in the 1960's hit, "Sittin' On the Dock of the Bay," by Steve Cropper and Otis Redding. A man left Georgia and ran away to San Francisco. Lonely, troubled, and hopeless, he sat on the dock of a bay, watching the tide roll away. The chorus says: "Look like nothing gonna change/ Everything still remains the same/ I can't do what ten people tell me to do/ So I guess I'll remain the same."[2]

The song has captured the lonely emotions of two generations because many people have thought about running away at one time or another. I've come to the conclusion that running away is not a bad thing. Leaving Georgia for San Francisco to sit on a dock watching ships roll in is a bit drastic, though, especially if you happen to have a job, a family, a mortgage, and a bit of a reputation. But when these components of life produce more stress than happiness, people have been known to do the irrational.

I don't recommend we do the irrational when life is pounding us like a rock crusher. I suggest we run away rationally, as Jesus did. The Gospel writers tell us that Jesus often pulled away from the crowds because he needed to be alone.

Anyone who works in a job that is people centered and service oriented understands the kind of emotional and physical energy expended in helping others. Today, most of our jobs are service oriented, compared to the physically labor-intensive jobs of generations past. When we give eight to ten hours of ourselves a day to other people, many of us discover we have nothing left to give our families or ourselves. The stress load can become so great that thoughts of running away multiply quickly. Years of this kind of stress can devastate a person emotionally. If we don't run away rationally, irrational behavior is bound to occur.

Jesus ran away rationally. He pulled away from the crowds to spend time alone. He prayed. He fasted. He listened to God. He gained perspective. He rested. He made plans. Then he reentered the world to minister again.

Do you feel the need to run away? Then you are in good company because Jesus made it a habit. He did not run away from his responsibilities or his calling. He ran away from the needs of others long enough to meet his own spiritual needs. He ran away for small segments of time and in the process, he was reminded of what he had to live for and what he needed to die for.

Matthew tells us that on one occasion after Jesus had dismissed a crowd, he went up on a mountainside by himself to pray. His position on the hillside gave him a view of the Sea of Galilee. As he sat there and prayed, Jesus must have watched the boats on the lake and one boat in particular, the one carrying his disciples. Later in the evening, a storm arose. The boat the disciples were in was a considerable distance from land and was being buffeted by the waves. Jesus walked out on the water to them. When he got into the boat with them, the waves quieted and the sea drew still.

Jesus didn't sing Otis Redding's song. Jesus embraced change, especially when he could change a person's fear into security, loneliness into comfort, sadness into joy, sickness into health, hopelessness into hope, and what is most important, disbelief into faith.

Jesus was emotionally and spiritually replenished through the time he spent alone with God, which seems to have given him the strength to reenter the world and bring about change in the lives of others, bringing them closer to the kingdom of God.

Does your situation look as though it will never change? Run away. Don't run away hopelessly. Don't run away to waste your time. Don't run away from responsibilities or your calling. Don't run away from your family or your friends. Rather, find moments of time during the day and longer stretches of time on other occasions to run away to be alone with God. Use the time to pray to God for guidance, strength, and perspective. Get away for a few days if possible. Chances are the chaos will still be present when you return. You may not come back walking on the water. But the time spent in the presence of Jesus, away from the demands and chaos of this world, will keep your boat from being sunk by the waves. Your fear will subside. A calmness in your spirit will emerge. You will see evidence of change occurring within yourself and then in the world around you, and you will be compelled to join with Jesus' disciples who said to him, "Truly you are the Son of God" (Matthew 14:33).

LOSING THE GOLD FOR GOING TOO FAST

I've got my sights set on the next Olympic Games. I've found a sport for the over-the-hill crowd: race walking. Race walkers walk as fast as possible without running. It's not as easy as it sounds. A racer is said to be walking as long as one foot is on the ground. If both feet come off the ground, one is said to be running and is warned twice before being disqualified. Some people question whether this event should even be an Olympic sport.

It would be more of a sport and certainly more interesting to spectators if racers were required to walk backwards. A skipping contest would be fun to watch as would a three-legged race with a partner. Race walking just doesn't seem to strike much excitement in people. So why does this sport interest me?

I have been in training for this event a long time. The days are so busy that one appointment merges with another. Days clip by at an accelerated rate. I race from one stage of the day to another, from one hour to the next, from day to day, month to month without being able to see the finish line. I know I'm not alone. I pass people during the week that are race walking. Sometimes I'm passed by others, which only makes me want to move faster.

In the 2000 Olympic Games in Sydney, Australia, Jane Saville, an Australian race walker, had the finish line in sight during the 200-meter final. She was in the lead when the judge raised the red flag that disqualified her. The judge saw both feet come off the ground. Her walk had turned into a run. She was disqualified from the race and lost the gold for going too fast.

That would probably be my fate should I make the Olympic Games. It's the problem I have in my training. I'm moving too fast. Admittedly, all I am doing seems good and the only way to do everything is to keep up the pace. When I look at the schedule and ask myself what should be cut out of the day, I cannot find anything I feel can be eliminated. In fact, the faster I walk, the more I find needs to be done and the more people expect me to do. Maybe you can relate. So what's the solution?

I need to pursue a medal in another discipline, like "still sitting." No Olympic medals are awarded for being still. It wouldn't be much of a spectator sport either. It doesn't require the physical strength of an Olympic athlete. But being still does require the mental discipline of an athlete. Disciplining oneself to focus on issues of the day and matters of the heart requires great spiritual discipline.

The Psalmist was a gold medalist in this field. He once wrote about his training philosophy:

> Delight yourself in the Lord and he will give you the desires of your heart. Commit your way to the Lord; trust in him and he will do this: He will make your righteousness shine like the dawn, the justice of your cause like the noonday sun. Be still before the Lord and wait patiently for him.
>
> —Psalm 37:4-7a

It's ironic—as I race through the week, I'm trying to accomplish what the Psalmist says the Lord will give to me if I remain still before him. How many red flags will be raised in front of me before I ever learn what the Psalmist knew so well?

TAKING DIRECTIONS FROM OTHERS

The pastor who traveled the Canopy Road placed his trust in his secretary to provide him the directions he needed to find an alternative route. Many of us, especially men, find it difficult to take directions from others. We believe in the sixth sense approach to finding the right turn.

Fortunately for all of us, the highways we travel are usually clearly marked. Signs along the way provide most of the necessary information to help us get to our destination. A key to finding our way is to know whom we should trust for information and where to look for the signs God places along the way for us to follow. God doesn't intend for his signs to be confusing, but clear and direct.

The directions the world gives us are much like the ones I get sometimes down South. Instead of being given highway numbers, street names, and the exact amount of mileage between turns, people in South Georgia give directions like this: "Well, you go down to where that old tobacco barn used to be and hang a right. You go a right smart ways up that road but not too far. You'll know you've gone too far if the road becomes a dirt road. When you see a big fish pond off to the left, go about another mile or two, and you'll come to a road off to the right. But don't take that road; take the next one. After you cross the second bridge, you'll take the next to the last road on the left. Start looking for the house. It's the only house with a porch on the back and there's a big black dog that always lies on the steps. You can't miss it."

Why is it that I always miss the house with directions like that? It's usually my luck that the barn's been rebuilt, the dirt road's been paved, the pond's been drained, the bridge has been replaced by a culvert, and the dog's asleep under the back porch, not on the front steps. No wonder men don't stop to ask for directions. We can get lost on our own. Why stop and ask someone to help us get lost?

Billy Graham tells of a time early in his ministry when he was in a small town to preach. Wanting to mail a letter, he stopped a young boy on the street and asked directions to the post office. When the boy had told him, Graham thanked him and said, "If you'll come to the Baptist church this evening, I'll be telling everyone how to get to heaven." The boy replied, "I don't think I'll be there. You don't even know how to get to the post office."[3]

Because most signs along highways have proven to be credible, people use them as aids in their travel. Inaccurate directions would cause people to lose trust in the information. The result would be confusion and frustration. Each motorist would be left to find his or her own way to the chosen destination. Think of the wasted time and energy such a lack of credible information would cause.

God doesn't want us wandering through life, left to our own sense of direction, confused, frustrated, wasting time and energy that can never be reclaimed. But that's the way many people live. You'd think that after following so many directions which have proven to be untrustworthy, people would stop following them. But finding our way through the maze of life is frustrated by our own sense of pride.

We either refuse to ask for directions, or the directions we received have been so poor and inaccurate that we simply fall back on our own resources. Eventually, many people come to the same conclusion as the writer of Ecclesiastes—that everything is "meaningless, a chasing after the wind" (Ecclesiastes 2:26b).

Little wonder the world is filled with signs directing people to lifestyles that promise to bring joy, happiness, fulfillment, and peace. Billboards, commercials, the internet, print media, and "friends" offer directions to these elusive yearnings. Most often, what's offered and found is pleasure as temporary as the morning dew which soon evaporates in the heat of the day. Like an addict needing another fix, people follow the same directions over and over only to find the same temporary pleasure which becomes less and less satisfying. The ultimate crisis for those living a life like this comes when the pleasure, or the pursuit of pleasure, becomes meaningless. A loss of hope often follows.

Jesus claimed to be "the way, the truth, and the life." He was more than a sign sent from God to show the world the extent of God's love. Jesus claimed to be the path to life—abundant life in this world and eternal life which extends to the next.

It's been my experience that those people who have walked this path and have followed Jesus have found the meaning and purpose they were searching for. I've known people who have followed religious signs only to become resigned that they were no more meaningful than the world's signs. But I've never known anyone who looked to Jesus daily as the way, the truth, and the life who has not found the path to abundant life and the road to heaven. Jesus has proven to be a credible sign and a credible path to life.

Jesus' simple invitation, "Follow me," which he often extended to others, is extended to us today. Following someone who knows the way is a lot easier than trying to figure it out on our own or getting lost with someone else's instructions. Either Jesus knows the way or he was a babbling fool whose directions will get us lost just like many other untrustworthy sources.

Which is he?

PASSING OVER THE MOST VALUABLE ITEM

As we find our way, it's easy to pass by valuable opportunities because we get caught up in a fast-paced world. Pastor Baker would have never taken the Canopy Road had he not been tricked into going that direction by his secretary. His rationalization would have been completely acceptable: "I don't have time in my day for detours." Interestingly, he took the detour only after his secretary convinced him that doing so would be a favor to her.

Finding our way requires that we find a good balance between taking care of others and taking care of ourselves. Care-givers like Pastor Baker often have trouble taking time out for themselves.

Other people are on the opposite end of the spectrum and have trouble making any decision that is not selfish in nature. In fact, more people are in this category. Genesis teaches us that this has been human nature since creation.

Several years ago, Reverend Ken Smith came to our church to conduct a revival. Each night before the revival, he met with the children in our chapel and told stories. He brought play money to give to the children each night. Sometimes he would give them a dollar for answering an easy question or just for trying. The difficulty of the question determined the amount of play money he gave them. Harder answers might push the reward up to ten dollars! The big payoff went to the child who could explain the main point of the biblical story.

The children came every night, excited and motivated. They listened attentively. Each night they lined their pockets with more money. More money meant more stuff they could buy from Ken's store which he promised to set up on the last night of the revival. Like kids waiting for Christmas morning, they waited impatiently for the last night of the revival when the store would open to purchase the candy and toys.

The picture of Jesus with a child on his lap and children at his feet was placed in the middle of $120 worth of merchandise from Wal-Mart. The small candy bars cost a dollar in play money. The Match Box cars sold for five dollars. The dolls sold for fifteen dollars. The ball and bat sold for twenty dollars. One by one, the children made their choices and used their play money to purchase the items which sported highly inflated prices to match the amount of money earned by the children.

The picture of Jesus with the children was in the middle of the table. The evangelist was going to give it to the first child who inquired about its cost. He was going to say, "I'm glad you asked about that picture. What do you think Jesus costs?" Perhaps the child would respond with a guess to which the evangelist would have said, "Child, Jesus doesn't cost you anything. All you have to do is ask for him." But no one asked about Jesus. Amid all the candy and toys, Jesus took a back seat. He was ignored.

The evangelist had taped a ten-dollar bill (real money) to the back of the picture which would have become the property of the child who asked about Jesus. The picture of Jesus was the most valuable item on the table and no one even picked it up. The most valuable item was free for the asking.

Too often, adults are just like these children. As we attempt to find our way, we get motivated when we have the opportunity to earn money to purchase toys. Our toys simply get bigger as we get older: a truck, a boat, a four-wheeler, a diamond, land, new furniture, a pool, a computer; the list is endless. What's wrong with these things? Nothing. But when Jesus is passed over in our pursuit of them we have broken the first commandment: "You shall have no other gods before me" (Exodus 20:3).

One way to help us maintain perspective is to heed the advice of the Psalmist: "Be still and know that I am God" (Psalm 46:10). When we stop and reflect on our journey, we have a chance of correcting our course. Otherwise we continue on the same path that usually involves trading time for money. We then trade money for things. If this becomes our primary pattern, we simply trade our life for things.

As you make your way through the store of life and view the many items for which you will give money or time, I remind you that Jesus is far more valuable than silver or gold. Jesus is more valuable than any other person you are living to please or impress. Jesus is more valuable than your career. Jesus is more valuable than success. Jesus is more valuable than your hobbies. We cannot afford to make the same mistake as these children who looked at all the goods of the world and forgot the Good News of the world — Jesus Christ!

The good news in a world with inflated prices is that Jesus doesn't cost us anything. It is true Jesus demands obedience, but to receive Jesus we can do no better than to open our hearts and invite him in—just as we are. This is the most important part of finding our way in life.

So in the midst of the wares laid before you today, I want you to see this picture of Jesus: "Here I am! I stand at the door and knock. If anyone hears my voice and opens the door, I will come in and eat with him, and he with me" (Revelation 3:19-20). That picture's worth more than a thousand words. Jesus felt it was worth his life. What's it worth to you?

WALKING THE LABYRINTH

1. Congratulations! You've turned off the fast paced world to read this book. Consider it your virtual labyrinth. You have been intentional in turning off the main road to engage in a spiritual journey. How often do you do this?

2. The Gospel writers indicate that Jesus often pulled away from the disciples for time alone where he could think and pray. If your life is too busy to spend time alone with God, your life is too busy. Walking this labyrinth indicates you are on the right path. Keep it up.

3. Do you find it easy to care for yourself? If you are a care-giver or work in a care-giving profession, it's likely that you care for others but find it difficult to care for yourself. Caring for yourself isn't sinful. In fact, if we are to love our neighbor as we love ourselves, then we must learn to take care of ourselves. What are you doing to care for yourself? As you find your way, what is something new or different you can begin doing for yourself that will also be pleasing to God?

4. Sometimes getting away for an extended period of time is difficult, if not impossible. A canopy road experience doesn't have to involve lengthy periods of time. What kinds of things might you do through a normal week that can create some canopy road experiences?

5. Life is lived at an extremely fast pace. It is easy to live so fast that we pass up what is most valuable in life. What is most valuable to you in life? If we say our family is most valuable, but in practice our family gets less time than the television, we are going to lose our way. If we say that God is more valuable than anything, but we spend more money on our hobbies than we do for the Lord's work, we are in danger of losing our way. If we say that our bodies are important because they are the temple of the Lord, but we do not exercise or eat healthy foods, we are in danger of losing our health. Saying that something is valuable in life doesn't make it so. Our actions must back up our words. Where do you need to shift gears and intentionally turn off the main road for a canopy road experience?

CHAPTER THREE

The Journey is filled with obstacles

REMOVING HARMFUL ROCKS FROM THE FIELD OF LIFE

"Gee!" yelled the old farmer as his mule dragged the plow through the crusty Georgia dirt. The mule pulled to the right and began to head for the barn. "Whoa! We ain't done yet," Lamar Abercrombie said to the mule. The mule relaxed, bending one leg slightly and lifting its hoof from the broken soil.

Lamar was a lean man, standing about six feet, four inches. He kept a close-cut beard and wore a straw hat with a green-tinted front brim that helped deflect the sun. He plowed in a long-sleeved shirt which he wore under his blue OshKosh overalls. He was so skinny that the slightest breeze would flap his clothes as if they were hung out to dry. He kept a plug of tobacco in his mouth or in the front pocket of his overalls for a quick retrieve.

Lamar walked over the terrace and kicked over a large rock that his blade had struck a few moments earlier. It was as large as a medium-sized watermelon. A firmly lodged rock could break or bend a good plow, so rocks were always moved from the field. It was heavy enough that he grunted when he picked it up. He carried the rock over to a grove of water oaks and deposited it in its resting place along with hundreds of other rocks that had been piled there through the years.

As many years as Lamar had plowed that field, he was still surprised every planting season when he ran across more rocks that needed to be moved. If he did not know better, he would have believed the field was actually growing new rocks.

To Lamar, the pile of rocks was sacred, an altar of sorts. Being a religious man, he remembered the many times the Bible speaks of the patriarchs and the prophets of God who built altars from stones they gathered from their surroundings, like the time Israel crossed the Jordan River bed while God held back the flow of the water with his mighty hand.

He recalled the passage in Joshua where the Bible says that "Joshua instructed men to gather twelve stones from the middle of the Jordan, one for each tribe of Israel. They carried the stones to their campsite for that evening. They used the stones as a marker for future generations" (Joshua 4:6).

Lamar first farmed the land as a teenager with his father. At that time, there were so many rocks that it seemed his father spent as much time saying "Whoa" to the mule as he did "Gee" and "Haw." Removing the stones was an inconvenient but a very necessary task which fell to young Lamar.

As the old farmer dropped one more rock onto the pile, his mind raced back to the days he worked the field with his father. He could remember how his father barked out orders to come and remove rock after rock. He remembered cursing under his breath, never letting his father hear him, of course, as he carried all those rocks to the edge of the field. Some days there were just too many rocks.

Lamar stood in the shade for a moment. He went over and dipped his bandanna into the jug of water he kept buried in a hole to keep it cool. He pulled out a biscuit and a piece of ham left over from breakfast and ate them while he looked at the pile of rocks.

He called out to his mule, "Lula Bell!" Through the years, Lamar had had more conversations with mules than with people. He'd discovered they were good conversationalists because they listened so well. "If that pile of rocks could talk, they'd tell you that I've been working this land for almost sixty years. Some of them might tell you the words I spoke as I carried them to their resting place, too. I'm afraid those words wouldn't be fit to hear, Lula Bell."

Occasionally he'd see a rock he recognized, remembering the very place in the field he'd moved it from. After finishing his biscuit, he walked back to his mule. He lowered his voice but continued to talk. "That's been a long time ago, Lula Bell. Why, I've gone through four mules in that length of time. You might be my last mule, Lula Bell."

He cut an apple in half and shared it with his working companion. "Come on," he said. "Back to work." Besides being a good listener, Lula Bell never complained about work, which was another reason Lamar was fond of his mule.

As he plowed the remainder of that day, it occurred to Lamar that his life was a lot like that pile of rocks. He remembered that as a young man he was determined to leave the farm as soon as possible so he could live his life the way that pleased him. He resented the structure of his home as much as a horse resents a bit the first time it's placed in his mouth.

Lamar left the first chance he got and lived exactly the way he wanted. As he grew into his early twenties, Lamar was a lost soul. His heart became hard, as hard as a rock. He was lost and didn't know it. He was almost thirty before he began to change.

As Lamar plowed, he thought about all the changing that had taken place in his life since those early days. As he plowed the field, he had a song of thanksgiving on his lips that God had kept on plowing in his life, kept on planting seeds, and kept on placing people in his path who helped lift the damaging rocks and set them aside.

As a young man, his drinking was a rock that broke many hearts. His temper was another rock that did lots of damage. The list was long. That pile of rocks reminded him of the sins that had been uprooted and were no longer a part of him. Some days when Lamar looked at that pile of rocks, he saw all that he used to be and it scared him. Sometimes he was even moved to tears as he thought about how God had continued to work in his life. God's pile of grace is always higher than our pile of rocks.

As he walked behind the mule, he prayed a prayer of thanksgiving for the many people the Lord had brought into his life who had helped remove the rocks before they broke off chunks of his life that could not be replaced or repaired.

Without a doubt, Lamar had grown into an exemplary citizen. He became a deacon in the church, a good husband, and a proud grandfather. He had mended fences with his children and his wife for being a drunk in the early years of their lives. Lamar's pile of rocks reminded him of the kind of person he used to be and, by the grace of God, the kind of person he had become.

Though he had come a long way, he knew his life was just like the field he plowed. A lot of progress had been made, but God kept running into new rocks as He plowed around in Lamar's life. Lamar kept thinking maybe one day they would all be gone. But he knew that wouldn't happen in this life. We grow new rocks that need removing.

Although he was disappointed in himself each time God pointed out another rock that needed to be removed, Lamar figured as long as God continued to break ground and expect him to bring forth a harvest, his life would have meaning and purpose.

It occurred to him that he should bring his grandchildren to visit that pile of rocks and tell them what it symbolized to him. Perhaps those rocks could serve as a testimony of thanksgiving to the Lord to future generations just as those rocks from the Jordan River reminded future generations of Israelites what God had done through Joshua as they entered the Promised Land.

Lamar spit some tobacco juice out the side of his mouth, one rock that had yet to be removed. He called out to Lula Bell, "Giddy up! Let's head to the house." She knew the way home. Thankfully, Lamar had learned his way home, too.

GETTING THE PAST OUT OF OUR EYES

After depositing another rock on the pile, the old farmer allowed himself to reflect on his boyhood when he spent long days removing rocks from the field. There's value in looking back so long as the past doesn't get in our eyes and cause us to lose focus on the job at hand. Past mistakes can be like rocks in the field. We need to deal with those parts of our life and move on.

Charlie Brown and Lucy are talking about the ball game. Lucy explains why she missed the ball: She says, "I remembered all the others I've missed . . . the past got in my eyes!"[4] How many times has the past gotten in your eyes?

A woman who reflects on her younger days remembers a relationship with a man which resulted in a pregnancy. She wasn't in love with the man. She did not feel prepared for motherhood so she decided to have an abortion. Years later she is saddened at the thought of having aborted the child. The decision seemed right at the time, but she often feels guilt about ending the pregnancy. She struggles to get the past out of her eyes.

An old man reflects on his relationship with his grown children. All his children are distant and have little to do with him because he mistreated their mother and paid little attention to them when they were young. He worked all the time and spent his spare time with his friends. Now, in his old age, he finds himself lonely, knowing he cannot undo what's been done. He cannot get the past out of his eyes.

Parents of a teenage son struggle with his rebellious ways. They argue with him a lot, especially when the son breaks curfew. He's drinking and maybe doing other drugs. One night in an argument the son says, "Tell me, what kind of teenagers were you? Didn't you sow some wild oats, too?" The parents are caught off guard. They deflect the question, but they later admit to one another that they are not proud of the lives they lived as teenagers and young adults and wonder if their past has affected the way they are raising their son. Their past has been brought back to their eyes.

A man in his fifties still has trouble sleeping. Though the war in Vietnam ended more than thirty years ago, he still finds himself in the jungle during his sleep. He sees the thick jungle foliage, hears the choppers, and feels the uneasiness that comes when you think you are being watched but never know for sure. He smells the aroma of a cigarette lit for a dying comrade. He struggles with the guilt of the killing he had to do in service to his country. He wakes up in the middle of the night in a cold sweat and wonders if he'll ever get the past out of his eyes.

Part of who we are is a combination of choices we have made and events beyond our control. We build on the positive parts of our past, but we struggle to get the negative parts of our past out of our eyes. Often we cannot live joyfully in the present nor have hope for the future because we cannot get the past out of our eyes.

God does not want us to be enslaved to our past; God wants us to learn from our past. But what is more important, God wants us to live in the present and have hope for the future.

The Old Testament story of Joseph is inspiring. As a teenager, Joseph was sold into slavery by his brothers, then carried away to Egypt. He spent many years in prison but was later released when his ability to interpret dreams proved valuable to the Pharaoh. Joseph learned to live in the present. God blessed him and through him God blessed all of Egypt. During the years Joseph was in charge of storing all the grain for the upcoming years of drought he had predicted, he and his wife Asenath gave birth to their firstborn, Manasseh, whose name means "God has made me forget all my trouble" (Genesis 41:51b).

Do you have trouble getting the past out of your eyes? The good news is that God can help you move beyond your past mistakes and beyond the bad chapters of your life to create chapters filled with new possibilities, new hope, and renewed joy. The good news is that our past does not have to dictate the future.

If one's past dictated the future, would God have used Moses to lead the Hebrews out from their slavery in Egypt? No. The blood on his hands from killing an Egyptian in an attempt to defend a fellow Hebrew would have kept him from being used of God.

If one's past dictated the future, would the prostitute Rahab have been able to save the spies, leave the city of Jericho with them, and change her life to become a strong symbol of faith in Hebrew history? No. She would have been doomed to a life of selling her body to survive.

If one's past history dictated the future, could Paul have stopped killing and persecuting the Christians to become a persecuted

Christian himself? No. Paul would have continued his misguided ways.

Referring to his past, Paul once wrote to Timothy that he considered himself the worst of sinners. "But for that very reason I was shown mercy so that in me, the worst of sinners, Christ Jesus might display his unlimited patience as an example for those who would believe on him and receive eternal life" (1 Timothy 1:16).

Even though Paul did not forget the past, Jesus helped Paul get the past out of his eyes and opened his life up to new possibilities. This fact is demonstrated in these words Paul wrote to the church at Philippi:

> Not that I have already attained, or am already perfected; but I press on, that I may lay hold of that for which Christ Jesus has also laid hold of me. Brethren, I do not count myself to have apprehended; but one thing I do, forgetting those things which are behind and reaching forward to those things which are ahead, I press toward the goal for the prize of the upward call of God in Christ Jesus.
>
> —Philippians 3:12-14 NKJV

God knows everything about our past. There is not anything in our past God cannot forgive or help us overcome. As long as the past is in our eyes, we will be like Lucy; we will miss many wonderful opportunities that come our way. The best way to get the past out of our eyes is to focus on Jesus. Jesus will help us identify those stumbling blocks in our way and deal with them so our future will be filled with great promise and possibility.

Ignoring Rocks Will Rock the Boat

The farmer didn't like the work of removing rocks from the field, but he knew from experience that to leave rocks in the field created a greater hardship and loss.

To ignore stumbling blocks on our journey causes problems that could have been avoided. Problems don't just go away. They may lie dormant, and when they rise they are usually bigger than before. It's important to deal with issues as they arise.

For example, I took the opportunity during the Christmas holidays one year to take my two sons to a Rotary Club meeting. As we neared the Country Club, we noticed a turtle attempting to make the treacherous journey from one side of the road to the other. That turtle had a problem. I could have ignored the problem, but for some reason my conscience was turned on high that day.

A turtle has some unique protection. When danger approaches, it simply pulls its head and feet inside its shell and rides out the storm—sort of the way a lot of people do when a hurricane or other bad storm approaches. Come to think of it, that's how some people handle their relational problems, too.

As I drove by that turtle, I knew his shelter wasn't going to be much of a match for an automobile, so we turned around, headed back for a rescue mission. I felt a little like Steve Irwin, that "Crocodile Hunter," going in dangerous terrain to rescue one of God's creatures. "Watch this, mates, as we pull off the road, weave between traffic, pick up this little fellow, and return him to the waters of the Country Club pond."

I pulled off the road. The turtle was just ten feet from us. One car passed, then two, and just as my son was about to get out for our great rescue—"flap-flap!"—some moron runs right over our turtle. Now I admit, it wasn't as traumatic as watching a dog or a cat get run over. All the same, we had a little bit of that Crocodile Hunter anger in us, as on those occasions when he goes to rescue an animal, only to discover that the locals have killed it before he got there.

As I drove on to the Country Club, it occurred to me that we were trying to rescue the same kind of animal we use as target practice in my father's pond in Alabama. With dozens of heads bobbing up to the surface like corks, we unload our twenty-two rifles with one goal in mind, to reduce the turtle population in Alabama.

Now isn't it strange how we can treat turtles so differently? Why would we take the time to try to save a turtle that's crossing the road in Georgia while we try to eliminate dozens that are minding their own business in my father's pond in Alabama? It's not the deepest of philosophical questions, but I was surprised where the answer carried me.

On some human level, we identified with that turtle crossing the road. The odds of surviving were not very high, and we wanted to help. On the contrary, all those turtles in my father's pond strike no emotional cord in us. We see them as a group of turtles, not as individuals. So what's the big deal if we take out a few? Who's going to care? Besides, reducing the turtle population might help the fish population.

As I said, that's not very deep until you apply this rationale to people. We tend to stereotype people when we view them in groups. We make blanket statements about another race, about people in a particular political party, about people whose religion is different from our own, about people from another country. We think they are all alike. We think they look alike and think alike. We don't care if our country develops policies that are detrimental to them or if we develop attitudes that demean them because, after all, we think we are right in our opinions.

Isn't it strange how all of that can change when we meet people from different races, religions, countries, or political parties who dispel our preconceived notions about what kind of people they really are? When we meet individuals with feelings like ours, hopes and dreams like ours, and families like ours, we feel a measure of shame and guilt regarding our previous misconceptions. Instead of taking aim at them, we surprisingly find ourselves drawn to them.

During the years following World War II, Americans hated the Japanese. Following the war, the Japanese were often portrayed as beasts rather than human beings. Stories from James Bradley's book, *Flyboys*, help us understand the reasons.

In his book, Bradley details the horrific fate of eight airmen captured by the Japanese on Chichi Jima, a tiny island 700 miles south of Tokyo, in September 1944. Bradley researched the fate of the eight airmen and discovered they were tortured, beaten, and then executed by beheading. Four of the men were carved up by the island garrison's surgeons and meat from their bodies was eaten by senior Japanese officers. Little wonder the Japanese were hated.[5]

One soldier who did not meet such a fate was Lieutenant George Bush, a twenty-year-old navy pilot who was shot down near the island and rescued by an American submarine, the *USS Finnback*, after his Avenger torpedo bomber was hit by Japanese anti-aircraft fire during a bombing raid on the island on September 2, 1944.[6]

In 1994 the former president returned to the island with CNN reporter Paula Zahn and was met there by a former Japanese soldier, a man President Bush had never met. This former Japanese soldier was responsible for guarding airman Warren Earl Vaughn, one of the eight "flyboys" killed on the island. Vaughn was kept at the radio station and used by the Japanese as a translator.

The former Japanese soldier told the story of how he and Vaughn became friends. He discovered that Vaughn was a very likable person. He was not at all like the Americans he had been taught to hate. Apparently, the American took some liking to his enemy as well. Some trust developed between them. Once, when escorting the American through the jungle, the Japanese soldier fell into a pit but was rescued by his American prisoner.

Then one day, unexpectedly, the order was given for the American to be executed. The Japanese soldier who had been guarding Vaughn protested vehemently, all to no avail. Losing his American friend brought such grief to this soldier that in honor of him, he renounced his Japanese name and took the American's name as his own, Warren Earl Vaughn. For the last six decades (at the time of the 1994 interview) this man has lived in Japan with his American name and with the memories of the atrocities done to this American, who surprisingly became his friend.

During the interview, Paula Zahn asked President Bush if his opinion of the Japanese would have been softened a bit had he known such a story following the war. President Bush admitted that it certainly could not have hurt.

Pilots and tank operators and artillerymen have to remove themselves as much as possible from the fate of those below or across the way. I suppose the enemy has to be treated as little more than turtle heads bobbing in a pond in order for some to carry out their objective. "There's a time to kill," as the Bible teaches in Ecclesiastes 3:3. I understand that without a measure of it we would not be a free country, enjoying life as we know it.

But to live as God intended, to live as Jesus instructed, loving our enemies, doing good to those who persecute us, we must learn to see those different from us as people with feelings much like our own, with hopes and dreams much like ours, with families much like our own. That happens when we see people as individuals, when we learn their names, when we learn to care what happens to them. When we cease stereotyping people and see them as individuals, surprisingly, we often find ourselves helping them instead of trying to eliminate them.

A little reflection on our past can help us recognize those we have stereotyped, those we have treated with disdain, and those we have treated as enemies without any attempt to love them as commanded by Jesus. Strained relationships are a huge stumbling block in life. If the stumbling blocks of strained and broken relationships are not removed, we will continue to run into the same issues over and over.

Pulling back into our shells, thinking the crisis is going to pass is a dangerous game. Sooner or later the practice is going to get us smashed. Ignoring the rocks in the field of life not only rocks the boat—it has the potential to sink the boat as well.

THERE WILL ALWAYS BE MORE ROCKS

Each year as the farmer plowed his field, he would hit more rocks. Each year he was surprised. He'd removed so many rocks and the land had been farmed so many times, he thought he would eventually remove all the rocks from the field. The thought had even crossed his mind that the field was actually growing more rocks.

In this story, rocks represent obstacles that can cause us harm as we seek to find our way. Everyone has a different list of chronic problems, and we all have to do battle with new rocks that constantly pop up in our lives.

Fear is a common stumbling block that many people deal with. Fear can keep us from doing the Lord's will.

Some time ago my sons told me about a stray dog that was frequenting our home. "He has a collar," one of them said. To him this meant the dog had a home and could simply have become lost. Still, I thought they were informing me about the dog so I could be the brave father and chase the dog away.

After my younger son was viciously attacked by a dog in Alabama, I joined him in being extremely cautious around dogs. In order to protect my children, I decided to treat all strays as threats. I have concluded that for my children's sake, it's best to treat all unknown dogs as potential maulers. Such an attitude doesn't allow much room for compassion to be expressed to stray dogs, but it keeps my boys out of the Emergency Room, so I don't lose much sleep over it.

One morning I walked out the front door, and this strange dog was lying on the porch. The dog did have a collar, but it had no identification. I had one agenda: send the dog on down the road to become someone else's problem. Though my conscience waved a guilty flag at me, I pegged the dog with a pine cone. He didn't get the message, so I found a stick big enough that would. I was motivated to move this dog on down the road by my fear of strange dogs and my desire to protect my children. Compassion has no room to operate in a heart filled with fear.

After driving the dog away, I was surprised that I was not welcomed as a hero by my children. In fact, they were angry with me. My older son informed me that he'd been feeding the dog, which explains why the dog had decided to camp on our front porch. Only then did my younger son suggest that we should have taken a picture of the dog and put it in the paper in order to find its real owner. Perhaps both of them remembered that we once took in a stray dog and made it our own, a dog which we kept for eight years. They were probably wondering what happened to that kind of compassion.

The experience left me confused. I thought I was justified in sacrificing compassion for the animal to insure the safety of my children. Isn't there a time when fear ought to override compassion? Who among us picks up hitchhikers, for example?

When the twin towers fell in New York City, our nation began to struggle again with the deep conflicting emotions of fear and compassion. If we live in a constant state of fear, it will become impossible to be compassionate to people without great discrimination in our choices. But if we don't learn to see the potential for danger in this world and seek to protect ourselves from it, we are sure to be bitten again.

Fear is a natural emotion which arises in response to a real or perceived threat. Aren't there times when the highest moral value has to do with protecting our family and our property without regard to compassion? Or is it possible to be afraid and yet choose to be compassionate?

As we struggle, we realize there are problems bigger than our ability to solve without creating other problems in the process. Such a realization ought to humble us and cause us to seek the wisdom of God in choosing our options and to accept the forgiveness of God when we choose wrong ones.

Life does have a way of creating new rocks that cause us to stumble. We never get our field so cleaned up that we will never hit any more rocks. Each stage of life offers a different set of circumstances that presents us with issues not presented in the former stage. Each new job, hobby, commitment, and opportunity will present its own set of rocks that will need to be removed so we do not stumble.

Fear is just one example of an emotion that can develop in light of new circumstances. Though fear can help protect us from potentially dangerous situations, it can also immobilize us. When fear becomes a stumbling block to us, may God help us to have the wisdom to know it. With the Lord's empowerment, we pray for the strength to remove the fear which keeps us from being compassionate to others and serving the Lord in the way He desires us to serve.

GOD'S PILE OF GRACE IS BIGGER THAN OUR PILE OF ROCKS

When my older son John was a young teenager, I helped him build a derby car from a block of wood for the Royal Ambassador derby race at our church. I wasn't too excited about the task since I (I mean we) usually produced a losing car. The cars other kids brought to this competition were Porsches to our Volkswagens.

We were putting the final touches on the car by bringing it up to its five-ounce maximum weight. I had a great idea of how to accomplish this task. I put some heavy fishing lead inside a light socket receptacle, which I held with some vise-grips. I melted the lead with a blow torch, and then poured the lead into the cavity we created on the underside of the car.

Now that sounds like a cool father-son activity! Actually, it wasn't cool – it was hot – really hot! Halfway through the process, an air bubble developed in the lead and it popped, sending some of the hot lead out onto my arm, which opened a compartment in my brain that stores words for just those kinds of occasions. I said "%$#$%" faster than I can blink an eye.

I was embarrassed. Here we were doing a church-related activity. We were supposed to be bonding. These were moments my son was supposed to look back on and think about his great dad who took time out to help him build a great derby car. Instead, he hears his father swear.

I didn't know what to say. *Maybe he didn't hear me,* I thought. I didn't look up. I just kept my head down and went about my job until my son broke the silence and gave me a blessing. "It's OK, Dad," he said. "Even preachers make mistakes sometimes."

Did I ever need that?! "Thank you, son. We sure do!" That was grace extended to a father by a son. That opened up the door for some conversation about swearing. It's not the last mistake like that I've made, but I know those words ought to stay buried in the brain and not be given permission to dance on the tongue.

The Bible says that "out of the same mouth come praise and cursing. My brothers, this should not be. Can both fresh water and salt water flow from the same spring?" (James 3:9-11). Paul wrote to the Colossians that they should rid filthy language from their lips (Colossians 3:9). The Bible seems clear on this issue.

This is a simple example of the "stuff" that we pile up along our journey. Along the way, we are going to miss the mark time and time again. But regardless of how many times we miss the mark, God is prepared to cover our mistakes should we repent and turn from our sin.

In describing the purpose of the law, Paul said to the church at Rome that "the law was added so that the trespass might increase. But where sin increased, grace increased all the more, so that, just as sin reigned in death, so also grace might reign through righteousness to bring eternal life through Jesus Christ our Lord" (Romans 5:20-21).

I like to paraphrase these verses like this: "God's pile of grace is bigger than our pile of rocks (sins)." The Lord loves to pile on grace. The key to finding our way is to experience the grace of God. Living under grace means we have found a way of life that offers such peace and serenity that we don't want to sin.

PASSING DOWN OUR FAITH

It occurred to the farmer that the pile of rocks could serve as an outdoor classroom for his grandchildren. When we sense we are on the right path, why keep it to ourselves? Just as we have learned from the journeys of others, we need to remember that others can learn from our journey as well.

Once we have discovered The Way, we must invite others to join us on the journey. The path is narrow and the gate is small, and only a few people will take us up on our offer. Nevertheless, in order to be true disciples of Jesus, not only should we be on the right path, but we should be working to persuade others to join us on our journey.

Christians are commanded to "go and make disciples of all nations, baptizing them in the name of the Father and of the Son and of the Holy Spirit, and teaching them to obey everything I have commanded you. And surely I am with you always, to the very end of the age" (Matthew 28:19-20).

As I look back on my childhood and teenage years, I can identify dozens of people who were significant in passing down their faith to me. One was my grandmother.

On my desk in my office, I keep a tattered Bible that belonged to her. I am honored to have it. When I was a child, I often saw this Bible lying on Grandmother's dresser or opened in her hands at home or at church. It was given to her by her father and mother in 1933 on her wedding day. Her father, The Reverend Fletcher M. Shirah, performed the ceremony at his home. The Bible was a fitting gift from a Baptist preacher to his daughter, one of eleven children. To my knowledge, it's the only Bible she used during her adult life.

Someone has said that a Bible that is falling apart is owned by a person who is not. This old Bible is indeed falling apart. Grandmother reinforced the cover with black electrical tape from my grandfather's tool box, leaving the words "Holy Bible" to show through on the binder. The leather that remains un-taped is cracking, revealing the paper backing underneath. The pages have turned to a dingy yellow and have an aroma that often accompanies old books.

Occasionally, I pick up her Bible and read from it, careful not to dislodge any pages. In reading from her Bible, I'm reminded that God's word was important to my grandmother.

She wrote a lot in her Bible, underlining key verses, many of which she had memorized. There are handwritten study notes on the back page. In the middle of the Bible are the names of her parents and all ten of her brothers and sisters, along with their dates of birth and, in some cases, deaths. Along with these is similar information about my grandfather's parents and all twelve of his brothers and sisters.

Spaced among the stories of the Israelites, the prophets, the stories of Jesus, and the early church are other treasures my grandmother kept close. There is a black-and-white photo of her parents in their old age. There is a copy of an order of service from Louisville Baptist Church, dated January 8, 1978. It's significant because on that Sunday, my father, John Helms, was ordained a deacon in his church. There's a bookmark with the picture of the mother Mary and the baby Jesus. There's a postcard-sized copy of a church covenant, published by the Baptist Sunday School Board. There's a page of notes written on a piece of stationery from the Louisville Pecan Company, where she did seasonal work for thirty years. There's a clipped article entitled, "Where Love Is, Sorrow Is." The article concludes with these words, "Sorrow is the price we pay for love and a fullness of life. The only way we could escape all sorrow would be never to have loved at all."

If we truly love others and we truly love the Lord, we must be intentional about passing down our faith to those around us and to those of the next generation. Some of the most important words of the Hebrew Bible for Jews and Christians are these:

> Hear, O Israel: The LORD our God is one LORD; and you shall love the LORD your God with all your heart, and with all your soul, and with all your might. And these words which I command you this day shall be upon your heart; and you shall teach them diligently to your children, and shall talk of them when you sit in your house, and when you walk by the way, and when you lie down, and when you rise. And you shall bind them as a sign upon your hand, and they shall be as frontlets between your eyes. And you shall write them on the doorposts of your house and on your gates.
>
> —Deuteronomy 6:4-9 RSV

This passage demonstrates an intentional nature of handing down our faith that is often neglected. It is true that children may learn more about the faith of their parents by observing their lives than by what their parents tell them about faith matters. Nevertheless, the Bible clearly shows that both faithful witness in lifestyle and verbal instruction are necessary for the proper development of faith. This is an important key to helping others find their lives.

Another Old Testament example is the time Joshua paused with the children of Israel after they crossed over the Jordan River into the Promised Land. Scripture says Joshua called the twelve men, one man from every tribe, and instructed them to cross over before the ark of the Lord and to take up a stone from the river bed. These stones were then used to make a monument that would be a sign among them and future generations.

61

When your children ask in time to come, saying, "What do these stones mean to you?" Then you shall answer them that the waters of the Jordan were cut off before the ark of the covenant of the LORD; when it crossed over the Jordan, the waters of the Jordan were cut off. And these stones shall be for a memorial to the children of Israel forever.

—Joshua 4:6b-7 NKJV

I miss my grandmother. If I could turn back the clock, I'd enjoy another quiet evening with her in her home, just the two of us. I'd sit at her kitchen table again, sharing some good conversation while I enjoyed one of her homemade biscuits loaded with pear preserves. Missing her is proof of my love for her. What sorrow I have in missing her is far eclipsed by all the love we shared and by the testimony of her quiet, faithful life, which she lived before her family.

Her Bible on my desk is a reminder of the simplicity of her life and faith. It reminds me of my roots, not only of family heritage but my spiritual heritage as well. Her Bible reminds me that her story cannot be told apart from her faith in God and her love for her family. The two became woven together like a piece of beautiful fabric. I pray I might clothe myself in such a way that my testimony shall not die even after my life is over.

The Apostle Paul wrote to his young friend Timothy reminding him that his faith in God was due in part to the faith of his grandmother Lois and his mother Eunice (2 Timothy 1:5). It's healthy to be reminded that our faith didn't originate with us and neither will the faith of the next generation originate with them. The faith of the next generation will have a lot to do with our own and how intentional we are about sharing how the Lord has impacted our journey.

When God is involved, we can even take the rocks we've stumbled over and use them as teaching points so others may not make the same mistakes as we. Those rocks can be turned into monuments that testify to the love, mercy, and grace of God.

WALKING THE LABYRINTH

1. When you discover something that needs removing in your life, do you take care of it right away or do you "plow around it"? What are the pros and cons of this practice?

2. Life changes quickly. On your journey, have the changes in your life brought you closer to God or carried you farther away?

3. Along your way, God has placed significant people in your path to bless you. Name the people that God has used to bless your life. Take the time to phone, write, or go see two of these people you have identified and be intentional about thanking them for what they have meant to you.

4. We are a product of the generations that have come before us. What spiritual impressions were left to you by previous generations of your family?

5. What legacy are you building that will be a lasting imprint on the generations that will follow you? This doesn't have to be anything monumental, but it does need to be something significant like being a good parent, volunteering your time

and skills within the community, or being a servant of God through the local church. What legacy would you like to begin to build? How will you begin building it?

6. Some days there are so many rocks it seems we are not making any progress. We question ourselves, "Am I spending more time removing rocks or plowing new ground?" Remember, the journey you are on wasn't promised to be an easy one. It takes commitment and resolve to pick up our cross and follow Jesus. As you walk this labyrinth, ask God for the strength to pick up your cross and follow Jesus. There's no better way to leave a legacy for future generations. There's no better life for you to live.

CHAPTER FOUR

pondering our mortality

THE SEED PLANTED ON GOOD FRIDAY

The wagon drove slowly through the plowed field carrying a casket with the body of John Chaney. The knoll on top of the hill was its destination, a small cemetery plot of the Chaney family. Strong oaks and a couple of sweet gums provided ample shade. Spring planters and fall harvesters often used the shade as a retreat from the hot South Georgia sun as they drank a swig of water from a gourd dipper or ate a sausage and biscuit left over from breakfast.

The graves on the hill were mostly ignored by the field hands. Occasionally someone from the Chaney family would walk through the field to bring fresh-cut flowers to place at the base of the crudely constructed headstones of Cecil Warren Chaney and his wife Gertie. There were a few small graves of their children, ages unknown. The oldest grave was that of Cecil Warren's brother, Cleve, who was killed in the Civil War. Etched in a piece of rotting-heart pine were the dates, 1847-1865. A few unmarked graves stood on the hill as well. Some said one belonged to a freed slave, but no one knew for sure.

John was the grandson of Cecil Warren Chaney. His death was unexpected. He took ill during the winter. A doctor from town treated him, but he did not improve. One night his fever spiked and never broke. Three days later he was dead. He was survived by his parents, a host of siblings, a wife, four children, and one on the way.

As was common in the early twentieth century, all the family lived close by. They were all present for the funeral. Family and friends walked behind the wagon and across the plowed field until they reached the shade trees. The limbs hung low as if they were bowing in respect to the family's loss. Reverend Shirah led the wagon carrying the casket and the procession until they reached the grave site.

The Chaney family wasn't the churchgoing type. Although several families had erected a one-room church near the Tallapoosa River, not many of the Chaneys made it a habit of going. John was the one exception. The preacher came on the first and third Sunday to preach, and John and his family rarely missed a service. He was a believer and had surprised his family by being baptized in the river following a Holy Ghost revival at the church.

Out of his eight brothers and sisters, only Roy, the youngest, attended his baptism. Roy was quiet. He listened a lot. John liked to talk a lot so the two of them complemented each other well. Some people thought Roy was a bit slow, but John knew differently. Time spent with a man helps determine another's character far more than rumors. They had spent many hours together planting seeds and harvesting crops.

One thing everyone agreed on—Roy was a hard worker. He could walk behind a mule for eight hours a day and still have enough energy and drive to work in his wood shop for four hours each evening, using kerosene lanterns for light on into the night.

As the casket was unloaded from the wagon, Roy felt pleased with his craftsmanship. Building it had helped him process his grief. For the first time in his young life, he pondered the meaning of life and death. He believed in God. Most folks did, he figured. But his older brother studied the Bible and tried to live according to what he read. It seemed to Roy that if God were aiming to pick one to leave this earth, he would have gone knocking on someone else's door. Why would God choose a loving husband and father, a man who sought to walk the narrow way, to be finished with life so soon?

Roy and a few of his brothers carried the casket to a freshly dug hole that members of the Tallapoosa River Baptist Church had dug for the family. The reverend began the service. He was an older man, someone Roy thought had seen more Sundays on earth than he had left.

Roy didn't know the reverend. He had met him at John's baptism, but they didn't speak. He didn't have much history with reverends so he held them suspect.

Roy's heart felt cold and calloused. He looked over at his parents and thought how unfair it was for them to have to bury an adult child. He looked over at John's pregnant widow and her children and thought how unfair life was for them to lose a husband and a father.

The reverend began to pray. Roy didn't close his eyes. Instead he looked out at the plowed field that had just been prepared for planting. He had plowed most of the twenty acres himself, John unable to help him as in years past.

Roy loved farming and thought there was something magical about dropping a seed in the ground and watching it grow to maturity. John used the word "holy" to describe the process, telling Roy that man could plant the seed but only God could make it grow.

"Amen," said the reverend as he finished his prayer. It was the only part Roy heard, but he listened to the reverend's first remarks. They were not very comforting but they were very true. He spoke of the harshness of life and of its brevity. "His wick was long," he said of John, "but his fuel ran out far too soon. We would have gladly given him some of our days, not only for his sake, but also for the sake of his wife and children. But we concur with Job that the 'Lord gave, and the Lord hath taken away'" (Job 1:21 KJV).

Roy was inclined to hold the taking away part against God. Roy didn't see any justice in these arrangements. When he looked into the faces of his nephews and nieces and John's pregnant widow, he found it hard to believe in John's loving God.

As if the reverend were reading his mind, he said to the family, "It would be hard to believe in a loving God, especially during times such as this, if we had not been introduced to God's love through his loving Son, Jesus. Not even Jesus was spared difficult times. A little younger than John, Jesus died a horrible death in his early thirties. Through the beatings, the death by crucifixion, Jesus felt abandoned by God. He cried out in a loud voice from the cross, 'My God, my God, why have you forsaken me?'" (Matthew 27:46).

The reverend looked at the family and said, "Today is the Friday before Easter. It is as sad a day for you as it was for the friends of Jesus on the Friday that he died. They were too full of grief to remember much Jesus had taught them. But later, one of Jesus' disciples, a man with the same name as the one we bury today, remembered these words of Jesus: 'Verily, verily, I say unto you, except a corn of wheat fall into the ground and die, it abideth alone: but if it die, it bringeth forth much fruit. He that loveth his life shall lose it; and he that hateth his life in this world shall keep it unto life eternal'" (John 12:24-26 KJV).

The reverend closed his Bible and spoke to the family and friends with sincerity and compassion. "Friends and family, I can't tell you why our friend John has died, but I can tell you on the authority of the Gospel that he has not died without hope. You don't have to live without hope either. You are farmers. You are people who are hopeful by nature. If you did not have a spirit of hope, you would not prepare your fields for planting each year."

The reverend walked over to Roy and asked him to hold his Bible. He walked over to the wagon and reached behind the rider's perch and brought out a small bag. He asked John's children to come forward and hold out their hands. He opened the bag and poured into their hands various kinds of seed.

"You know what these are, don't you? These are seeds we are getting ready to sow in the garden. Inside these seeds life is waiting to burst forth. But before this life can come, these seeds have to be buried and they have to die. In a month or two, you will not be able to find these seeds any longer; only their husks will remain. In dying, they will give rise to new life. This new life will be your hope through the spring, through the summer, and into the harvest."

He then turned to the adults and said, "Today is a day of grief on the Christian calendar because it is the anniversary of Jesus' death on the cross. This is also a day of grief for this family. But don't forget about Easter. Easter was the day Jesus was brought back to life. The Bible says, 'But now is Christ risen from the dead, and become the firstfruits of them that slept' (1 Corinthians 15:20 KJV).

"This verse means there is hope for John, that though he has died, he will yet live again. Again from the Word of God are these words of Paul to the Thessalonians: 'But I would not have you to be ignorant, brethren, concerning them which are asleep, that ye sorrow not, even as others which have no hope. For if we believe that Jesus died and rose again, even so them also which sleep in Jesus will God bring with him' (1 Thessalonians 4:13-14 KJV).

Walking among the family members, the reverend looked at each one with loving and caring eyes. He said, "The Lord will come for each of us one day. Some of us will be ready. Some of us will not. John was ready. Oh, no, he wasn't ready to leave here, to leave you, to leave his wife and children, but he was ready to receive the final part of his gift of eternal life. The good news, made possible by the events of Easter, is that God will raise those in Christ Jesus to new life. That's the difference Easter makes. But Easter will not come for you unless you are willing to give your life to Jesus."

The reverend then recalled the day that John came to Christ after hearing the gospel. He told of the joy he had in baptizing him in the river and the testimony John gave as he stood dripping wet in the Tallapoosa, citing his desire to see other members of his family come to know the Lord.

Skeptics and believers alike looked across the field as the preacher's voice rose and fell in a singsong cadence. Many of them pondered whether they should dare believe that death is not the end and that new life is possible beyond the grave. Looking into the darkness of the freshly dug grave gave some of them reason to doubt. Others from the church had affirmed many parts of the reverend's message with a smattering of "amens." Like a cow chewing its cud, some, like Roy, chewed on the reverend's words slowly and deliberately, pondering his message.

With the ending of the message, the reverend said, "Let us pray." Roy didn't bow his head. Instead, he looked at the plowed field. He looked at the bag of seeds the reverend had poured out for the children. He looked at the worn Bible he still held in his hands. He thought about his brother's faith.

Of all the years he'd planted seeds, he'd never thought about his work being an act of faith, an exercise in hope, an example of death and new life. Maybe his brother was right: planting seeds and watching them grow to maturity wasn't magical but was something holy, something God ordained, a tiny miracle, an example of the greater miracle God performs in every person who lives by faith.

Roy's eyes returned to the open Bible. As if by providence, his eyes fell on Hebrews 11:6: "But without faith it is impossible to please him: for he that cometh to God must believe that he is, and that he is a rewarder of them that diligently seek him" (KJV).

His brother was a person of faith. The reverend said he had received an eternal reward because of his faith. He had faith when he planted a field, and he had faith that the Lord would give him a home in heaven one day.

Though they occasionally spoke of spiritual things, Roy had never thought much about being a person of faith, until that day. After helping lower the casket into the ground, he left the cemetery without speaking to anyone.

At the edge of the field, he stopped and looked over the freshly turned dirt. He looked back up the hill at the freshly dug grave. He thought about the reverend's words about seeds and new life. He said a simple prayer and headed for his workshop. He didn't yet have his brother's faith, but the seed had been planted.

BELLY-UP IS NOT A GOOD SIGN

Eventually, everything that lives dies and returns to the earth. This lesson of life can be a shocking reality for a small child.

When my son Ryan was eight years of age, his hamster, Rocky, died. Ryan had grown quite fond of his hamster. He would take Rocky out of his cage and let it run around in his room. He enjoyed getting him out and showing him off to people who came for a visit. Unfortunately, Ryan did not take very good care of his furry little friend. It did not take a Sherlock Holmes to discover the cause of Rocky's death. There was no water in the water dispenser and no food in the food bowl. The poor little fellow starved to death!

Part of the benefits of children having pets is that they learn important aspects of life such as responsibility, love, and even grief. When pets die, a child learns that all creatures eventually die, sooner rather than later if they are not fed. A child's grief in the loss of a pet is a dress rehearsal for the deeper grief that life will surely bring.

I'll never forget the day we buried Rocky. I dug a hole for the little fellow while Ryan held him gently in his hands. I was tempted to eulogize him, but Ryan did not seem to be in the mood for sarcasm. When it came time to place Rocky in the hole, Ryan pitched him in the hole with more anger than fond affection. Anger is a stage in the grief process, but I'd not seen it expressed in quite that manner. Ryan cried most of the afternoon. I tried to be a consoling father. I knew I could not take his pain away. I just held him and listened to him. That's usually the best care we can give those who are grieving, whether it's a child grieving over the loss of a pet or someone experiencing the depths of grief in the loss of a close friend or a loved one.

Several years ago betta fish became very popular. The fish are able to live in unoxidized water for a long period of time. Many people enjoy these fish because of their beauty and the little care they require.

A few years ago, I visited an older member of our church. I noticed her betta fish and the lily growing in the water displayed on her coffee table. As we shared conversation, I noticed that the fish never swam around in the water. It just stayed in one place, which is not unusual for this fish. Upon leaving, though, I squatted down for a closer look. As I did, I could tell that the betta had lost its beautiful color and for good reason—the fish was dead. It was deceiving because the fish was supported by one of the roots of the lily. In fact, from a distance, it looked as if it were alive. Its bulging "bug eyes" were a good hint that the betta's swimming days were over. I hated to deliver the bad news but I told my elderly friend and her daughter that I thought the fish was dead.

With tones of denial in their voices, they peered for a closer look. I thumped the side of the vase and it dislodged the fish from the roots, and it made what appeared to be a graceful swim to the top. "There he goes. He's not dead," the lady said with relief. But once the fish made it to the surface, it turned belly-up. As you know, "belly-up" is not a good sign. After such a wonderful visit, I left feeling like the Grinch Who Stole Christmas.

There are many people like that betta fish. They are supported by the root systems of work, family, and leisure life. To the casual observer, these people are alive and well. However, outward appearances can be deceiving. Though people show many signs of physical life, a closer look will reveal that some people are spiritually dead.

In fact, the Bible teaches that before people become Christians, we are dead in our transgressions and sins. We may fool other people with what appears to be graceful swims through life's reefs and caverns. We might even dive into religious waters, fooling ourselves and others that we have life. However, we cannot fool God.

Jesus met his friend Nicodemus on one occasion to discuss matters of faith. Few people were more religious than Nicodemus, a Pharisee and a member of the Sanhedrin, the most important religious group of his day. Jesus told Nicodemus that "no one will see the kingdom of God unless he is born again" (John 3:3). Nicodemus' religion was not enough.

Though we are all made in the image of God, not all of us are alive in Christ. To be alive in Christ, to find our way in this life and into life eternal, we must experience a new birth in Christ. Until then, we are dead in our transgressions and sins. Our eyes are glazed over, and we can easily fail to recognize the state we are in. This is the work of Satan, the real Grinch in this world.

To others we may look alive, and some will even comment about how gracefully we are swimming through life. But unless we are born again, the Day of Judgment is coming when it will be apparent that the graceful swim to the top was really a dead life that turned belly-up, with no life and no hope.

The Good News is that even when we are dead in our transgressions and sins, we are loved by God. Because of God's love for us and because God is rich in mercy, God wants to make all of us alive with Christ, a free gift offered to each of us. Whether we accept the gift is a choice God leaves to us.

Sometimes it takes the death of someone we love to force us to contemplate the brevity of life, to force us to work out what we believe about this life and the life hereafter, and to think seriously about our own mortality. In the story, "The Seeds Planted on Good Friday," Roy began to contemplate some of the deeper meanings of life for the first time. Until we ponder our mortality, it's doubtful we will be able to live life to its fullest.

LIVE LIKE YOU WERE DYING

In November 2003, Tim McGraw's song, "Live Like You Were Dying," won song of the year and single of the year at the Country Music Association awards. The song is about a man in his forties who discovers he has a short time to live. Instead of feeling sorry for himself, he goes out and has every kind of positive experience he can with whatever time he has left.

The power of the song comes as this man ironically discovers a joy in life such as he's never had, even though he knows his time to live is short. In his song, he sings these challenging words: "Someday I hope you get the chance to live like you were dying."

I don't know whether McGraw's song has the power to change lives but it has a powerful message to those who live life as if they will never die. If we live as if we will never die, our lives need to be changed because chances are we are living for the temporal and not for the eternal.

Every day we exchange part of our lives for something. According to William E. Thorn, a man who lives seventy years can expect to spend twenty-three years and four months of it asleep, nineteen years and eight months at work. (Some people can do both of these at the same time.) He will spend ten years and two months in religion and recreation, six years and ten months eating and drinking, six years in traveling (that's got to be much higher if you live in Atlanta), four years in illness, and two years getting dressed (I'm guessing four if you are female. Of course, the extra time is noticeable). If the average television consumption is twenty hours per week, a person living seventy years spends more than eight years in front of the television.[7]

Would we change the way we live if we knew we were dying? Guess what—we're all dying! The only difference is that some of us have longer to live than others, but none of us knows how much time any of us have. Sooner or later, the obituary column will carry our names.

I believe McGraw is on to something with his song. If we lived like we were dying, many of the things we view as important would become trivial. If we lived like we were dying, many of the things we never get around to doing, we would do. McGraw sings, "I was finally the husband that most of the time I wasn't/ and I became a friend a friend would like to have/ and all of a sudden going fishin'/wasn't such an imposition/and I went three times that year I lost my Dad/Well, I finally read the good book/and I took a good long hard look/at what I'd do if I could do it all again."[8]

Jesus once told a parable about a man who became rich as a farmer. One year his crop was so bountiful that he couldn't store all his grain, so he tore down his barns and built bigger ones. Now he had life made, and he said to himself,

> "Soul, you have many goods laid up for many years; take your ease; eat, drink, and be merry." But God said to him, "Fool! This night your soul will be required of you; then whose will those things be which you have provided?" So is he who lays up treasure for himself, and is not rich toward God.
>
> —Luke 12:19-21 NKJV

The farmer lived his life as if he'd never die. That's a recipe for disaster with eternal implications. If we lived like we were dying, we'd be less materialistic and more concerned about our fellow man. We'd be less selfish and more giving. We wouldn't take life for granted. Rather, we'd wake up with thankful hearts for the gift of a single day. We would be less busy and more likely to notice the beauty of a rose or be more willing to sit with older people and hold their hands and listen to them share whatever's on their minds. If we lived like we were dying we would be more intentional about saying "I love you," and we'd try harder to settle our differences with our neighbor. If we lived like we were dying, we'd be less concerned about our earthly bank account and more concerned about storing treasures in heaven.

PONDERING OUR MORTALITY

In the story, "The Seed Planted on Good Friday," the death of his brother John forced Roy to ponder the existential questions of life. For the first time, he contemplated what being a person of faith was all about. After helping lower the body of his brother into the ground, he thought about the reverend's words about seeds and new life. He said a simple prayer as he headed home, and the seed of faith was sown in his heart.

Finding our way in life eventually causes us to face our own mortality. Facing our mortality is one of the most important parts of our journey in life. Our focus in life is likely to be on those things which are temporal rather than eternal if we live in denial that we are mortal.

Death is not a topic many people are comfortable discussing or even a topic we like to reflect upon. Not discussing death or refusing to reflect upon our own mortality will do nothing to keep it at bay. Since death is a part of life, we must make death a part of our inward journey because such a process will have an impact on where we place our values and what we choose to do with our lives.

Although some Protestant churches incorporate Ash Wednesday services into their liturgical worship calendar, very few people of my denomination (Southern Baptist) have participated in such a service or even heard of it.

Ash Wednesday is the beginning of the season of Lent. This day comes forty days (excluding Sundays) before Easter. In some traditions, the palm fronds used from the previous year's Palm Sunday services are burned and the ashes are used the next year for the Ash Wednesday service.

During an Ash Wednesday service, people come forward to have ashes placed on their forehead in the sign of a cross. The minister or priest uses his/her thumb to form the cross with words such as "Remember, thou art dust and unto dust thou shalt return," or "Ashes to ashes; dust to dust," based on God's words to Adam in Genesis chapter three. The primary purpose for this service of worship is to prompt people toward penitence and to reflect on our mortality. We don't have forever to seek forgiveness of our sins. One day we will all face the Great Judge, a day when the sheep are separated from the goats, a day when the Lord will open the Lamb's Book of Life to see if our name is recorded. Ash Wednesday reminds us that we have a limited amount of time to repent—for once we die, we face judgment.

When we face our mortality, we should be moved to face our beliefs about life and eternity. Just as important, we should be moved to face our reasons for living. As we do inventory through a season such as Lent, significant spiritual growth can come if we inventory whether we are living for the reasons the Lord placed us on this earth or living only for ourselves.

GRIEVE, YES, BUT GROW FROM YOUR GRIEF

Nothing prepares us for death quite like death itself. We hear rumors of death's effect upon people. We see it at a distance and know that people hurt and grieve. But until death knocks on the door of our home, until the chilling call of death is answered by someone we deeply love, we don't know death at all. Unless death comes for you early, eventually the death angel will knock on your door and take someone you love and grief will be as real for you as it was for Jesus' friends, Martha and Mary, when their brother Lazarus died.

One of my favorite verses of the Bible is John 11:35, "Jesus wept." It's important to me because it shows us that our Lord Jesus cares about our grief. Even though Jesus knew of the joy he was about to bring to this family in raising Lazarus from the dead, his heart was filled with empathy for his friends Martha and Mary as they wept for their brother.

People from various cultures, ethnic groups, and religions affix different meanings to the experience of death. However, grief is a universal emotion. If you've never experienced deep grief, the following paragraphs give one person's perspective of how the loss of a loved one affects every aspect of life.

In 2003, Andrea Tew lost her husband Eric to cancer. Three small children lost their father. As a part of her own therapy, Andrea kept a journal of her family's struggle to find their way through uncharted waters of loss and grief. Through e-mail, Andrea allowed many of us a very rare look into the soul of a person willing to be vulnerable, honest, and forthright with her feelings and emotions about disease, loss, death, and grief. I pray that this sampling of Andrea's words will bring you comfort and will help you find your way through any loss or grief you may be experiencing.

I have often wondered which would be worse—to lose a loved one suddenly, without warning, or to lose a loved one after an extended illness. I know that some extended illnesses can be long and hard on the patient and the family. However, I am thankful every day that Eric's death took place over an extended period and not suddenly. I know that I am going through the grieving process now. And part of that process is unpredictable—down one week, up the next. But I feel like I was also given the wonderful opportunity to do a lot of my grieving alongside of Eric.

Although we did not spend every moment of every day talking of his death or our love for one another, we were able to go through stages of grief in which we were able to grieve the loss of the life we once had, the possible loss of one another, and the loss our children would have to endure. I have realized that this grief will always be a part of my life. I will manage it in different ways as I pass through different stages, but I do not believe it will ever completely go away. I will learn to live with it, yet I will always carry it. My life, like it or not, will never be the same.

It changed even before Eric died. It changed on April 28, 2002 when the surgeon sat across from me and confirmed what I had dreaded so. I will never have the love of my life again on this earth. We will not grow old together. We will never be able to do just the simple, mundane, everyday activities of life together again. I will never be able to ask his opinion on things. My girls will not have their daddy to walk them down the aisle as they marry the love of their lives. My son will not take his first hunting trip with his daddy. But in many ways, it also changed for the better.

I now think a little longer before I get so angry about such stupid, insignificant problems. I consider other people's feelings more now. I have a deeper walk with God now. What I used to consider a major catastrophe isn't such a big deal anymore. I have a new measure for "having a bad day."

I was able to see my husband in a way that I would have never seen him had we not walked this path together. I have met people and had opportunities that would never have been mine had I not faced this trial. I can easily dwell on the negatives of this change in my life. But in order to survive, in order to make some sense of life again, I must focus more attention on the positives. I must learn to grow through this process. Grieve, yes, by all means, but also grow.

Andrea's words are challenging. They are a reminder that most of us will not make it through life without significant loss. If we do, it means that someone will be grieving losing us prematurely. Grief is a part of life. We have no choice about experiencing loss. In time, everyone loses someone or something meaningful. We can only hope that it comes later in life and not early.

Regardless of when it comes, the choice we are left with is how we will respond to grieving times. Will grief consume us? Will we be swallowed into its dark abyss and never emerge? Do we conclude that we will never be happy again? Will we allow ourselves permission to cry and mourn? Will we become and remain angry at the world and at God because our lives have been forever changed?

God created us with the capacity to grieve. Though the emotion is very healthy, we can get stuck in various stages of grief, cutting off the growth process so necessary for us to find joy, peace, and meaning as our lives continue.

Jesus taught Martha and Mary that even in the midst of grief our faith in God can grow. Because of Lazarus' death, Martha and Mary had an opportunity to grow in their faith in Jesus. Those mourning with them had the same opportunity, witnessing Lazarus come forth from the grave as Jesus called him out.

Lazarus eventually died again. Jesus' miracle didn't spare the family of Lazarus from future times of grief. Nor will our Lord spare us from grief. We will grieve at significant loss. But will we grow? Will we look for the good amidst the bad? Will we allow God to mold and shape us into the persons He wants us to be? God can use a time of grief as clay in His hands to shape a grieving experience into something useful in our lives. That's not to say that life will be the same. It is to say that God can take significant loss, even death, and help us to find hope, peace, and eventually joy.

I have never experienced grief to the depth that Martha and Mary were experiencing at the loss of their brother Lazarus or to the depth that Andrea and her children have experienced at the loss of a husband and a father. But I know if I live long enough, grief of this depth will likely come to me. It will come to us all. When it comes, how will I respond? I hope my faith will allow me to respond with the same fortitude and optimism as Andrea Tew. She writes:

It is hard for me to imagine the future now, because I cannot imagine it without Eric. But at the same time, there is a certain anticipation to see just how God is going to provide for us spiritually, physically, and mentally. I want my children to be able to look back when they are much older and be able to see how God carried us through a difficult time in our lives. Without the promises that God gives us, that desire could never be fulfilled.

But, because we know He holds our future in His hands, we can trust Him to see us through.

"May the God of hope fill you with all joy and peace as you trust in Him so that you may overflow with hope by the power of the Holy Spirit."

—Romans 15:13

May this be especially true during times of grief.

MY EPITAPH

It is my request to be buried in the cemetery at Prospect Baptist Church in Barbour County, Alabama when I die. I don't care to go there any time soon, but I know that this body of mine is temporary.

Prospect Baptist is the church of my early childhood. It was established in 1888. Like many old country churches, it has a cemetery adjacent to the building. It is reported that the first grave was that of a prospector who came to the area looking for work. He died, and no one knew anything about his family. Perhaps with a little guilt of not knowing this man and a vow to reach out to all who came their way, the members named the church for him, Prospect Baptist.

As a boy, I used to play among the graves of that cemetery between Sunday School and the preaching service. I would read the names of ancestors I had only heard about and visit the graves of a few people I had actually known. Most of the people buried there were unknown to me. Even so, names, dates, the designs of the memorials, and the epitaphs fascinated me, especially epitaphs.

Over the years I've collected a few epitaphs from cemeteries and have pondered what I might want scratched on a tombstone one day as a witness to stranger or friend who might pass by my grave. Here are a few I wouldn't want:

"Beneath this stone, a lump of clay, lies Arabella Young/ who upon the twenty-fourth of May began to hold her tongue." Sounds as if her epitaph was one thing in which Arabella didn't have a say.

"Here lies John Smith, a politician and an honest man." Upon reading this epitaph, one woman is reported to have said in all seriousness, "Good heavens, isn't it awful that they put two people in the same grave?"

How about this one? "I told you I was sick."

A common epitaph found in many older cemeteries is scratched on the headstone of my sons' great-great-grandfather: "Kind friend, think of me as you pass by/ As you are now so once was I/ As I am now so shall you be/ Prepare for death to follow me."

With some humor, after reading this epitaph, one man replied, "To follow you I'm not content/ until I know which way you went."

There is much wisdom in that epitaph and even in the humorous response. We become so busy living and accumulating possessions and setting earthly goals that we forget death is coming.

Rarely is there a day when obituaries are not listed in my hometown paper, *The Moultrie Observer*. Reading obituaries is an interesting exercise. One notices that some people have had a rather lengthy stay on this earth by our standards. Others hardly had time to pitch their tents before the cool winds of death swept them away. Some have large families, others small ones. Some have a long list of accomplishments and others few. One thing they all have in common: they are dead. The final chapter in this life is written.

The Psalmist had a realistic view of life and death: "As for man, his days are like grass. He flourishes like a flower of the field; the wind blows over it and it is gone, and its place remembers it no more" (Psalm 103:15).

In contemplating his own mortality and that of others, the author of Ecclesiastes became discouraged and even depressed because he could not see where death treated the fool any differently than the wise:

For there is no more remembrance of the wise than of the fool forever, since all that now is will be forgotten in the days to come. And how does a wise man die? As the fool! Therefore I hated life because the work that was done under the sun was distressing to me, for all is vanity and grasping for the wind."
—Ecclesiastes 2:16-17 NKJV

Jesus had a different word to his disciples.

> Let not your heart be troubled; you believe in God, believe also in Me. In My Father's house are many mansions; if it were not so, I would have told you. I go to prepare a place for you. And if I go and prepare a place for you, I will come again and receive you to Myself; that where I am, there you may be also. And where I go you know, and the way you know.
>
> —John 14:1-4 NKJV

Do you know the way? Thomas was honest enough to say to Jesus, 'Lord, we do not know where You are going, and how can we know the way?' Jesus said to him, 'I am the way, the truth, and the life. No one comes to the Father except through Me' (John 14:5-6 NKJV).

A stroll through a cemetery can be a sober reminder of the brevity of life on this earth and a challenge to focus on what's most important in life, which according to Jesus is loving God with all of our heart, soul, mind, and strength and loving our neighbor as we love ourselves. If our daily focus is on these two endeavors, not only are we living an abundant life now but we are preparing for death and the life that follows. This is truly one of the most important keys to finding our way.

So here's the epitaph I'd like on my tombstone, "He Was Prepared—Are You?" I hope I can live in such a way to make this a true statement of my life, however brief or long my life may be. As others pass by my grave, perhaps they would be prompted to think of their own mortality and whether they are ready to stand before the One who will separate the sheep from the goats—the one who will say, "Well done, thou good and faithful servant," or "Depart from me for I never knew you."

BY FAITH HE STILL SPEAKS, EVEN THOUGH HE IS DEAD

Julie walked through the maze of graves at Mt. Sinai Primitive Baptist Church. She zigzagged between headstones, walking part of the time along the marbled edges of a grave's border, stopping occasionally to read the inscription on a tombstone. "Wilbur Jones. Born 1873. Died 1945." She quickly did the math. Seventy-two years of age at death. *That's a nice long life,* she thought.

Then it occurred to her that her own mother was sixty-seven: strong, determined, active. The word "old" hadn't even entered into her mother's vocabulary. In fact, she wouldn't attend the senior citizens' meetings at the church because she didn't count herself as a senior. As Julie left Mr. Jones' grave behind, she quickly rethought the age that she might call "old."

Julie was in the cemetery at Mt. Sinai doing some research on her family tree. She had become interested in genealogy and had been told that Sidney Perkins, her great-great-grandfather, was buried at the cemetery. She had never spent much time in a cemetery. She had attended only a few funerals and had never lingered afterwards.

As she walked through the graves, she found the small ones intriguing. *The child mortality was obviously higher years ago,* she thought to herself. It wasn't difficult to find graves of children sprinkled among those who had lived long productive lives. More times than not, the child's name was not included on the tombstone. Instead, it simply read "Infant child of," followed by the names of the parents.

Near one of the children's graves, Julie sat down on an old iron bench to catch her breath. The cemetery was quiet and peaceful. It was far enough away from the main highway that the traffic could not be heard.

The birds had the cemetery to themselves. Their songs were beautiful. Julie thought it was a bit ironic that their songs fell among people who could no longer appreciate them, at least as far as she knew. Their melodies lifted her spirits and even made her feel a bit guilty that she had to go to a cemetery to appreciate beauty that was around her every day. She even closed her eyes and allowed herself to drift away for a while—five minutes, maybe ten.

The same birds that helped put her to sleep eventually woke her up. A couple of mockingbirds seemed to be having some kind of disagreement in the tree that grew on the fence-line of the cemetery. She got up and walked a bit closer and discovered that the birds were diving at a snake that was up in the tree. She could see the bird's nest in the fork of one of the branches. There was no way of knowing whether the snake's presence had been discovered by the birds before or after the snake had helped itself to their eggs.

Having momentarily forgotten the real reason for her trip to the cemetery, she went back and sat down on the bench. She watched as the birds continued to dive at the snake until they finally knocked it out of the tree. She wasn't alarmed. Her brother often caught snakes when Julie and he were children. She could identify most snakes in the area. This snake was no threat, except to the eggs in the bird's nest.

As she sat there in a meditative moment, she remembered that the previous week's sermon she had watched on television was about the serpent from the second chapter of Genesis. Julie's theology was more liberal than her parents'. She interpreted the Garden of Eden story more as a parable than as a literal event. Talking snakes just didn't sound as if they belonged to a world of reality. Actual event or not, Julie was still careful not to miss the important meaning of the story and the point of the preacher's message: the serpent offered life but peddled death.

In that cemetery, Julie was surrounded by graves. Seeing the serpent trying to rob a nest of eggs reminded her of a Scripture verse she had memorized during her youth. Jesus said, "The thief cometh not, but for to steal, and to kill, and to destroy: I am come that they might have life, and that they might have it more abundantly" (John 10:10 KJV).

She looked around at all the graves. She wondered how many of those in the cemetery Satan had managed to steal. She bowed her head and began to pray. She gave God thanks that her life was already in his hands.

Having grown up in the country, Julie had sat under the preaching of several preachers. None of them ever stayed longer than two or three years. Most of them were not seminary trained. Their messages were not polished. The preachers were not well read except for the Bible, but they could quote more Scripture than most people had read. What they lacked in knowledge, they replaced with passion. Though occasionally a preacher seemed to be full of himself, mostly the church was blessed with humble men who preached a simple gospel. As a child, Julie gave her life to Jesus. She was baptized in a lake at a state park near the church. She knew her soul wasn't within reach of Satan. She had never doubted her salvation.

Even so, she knew she had drifted from her roots. Even though her mother and father brought her through the doors of the church whenever they were opened, Julie and her husband Greg were not so faithful. In fact, they were out of church more often than they were in. Greg played golf on most Sundays, and the children slept late. Julie sometimes curled up on the couch with a cup of coffee and watched a sermon on television. She knew this didn't help her children, but it was so nice to have that quiet time to herself.

As she sat on the bench, she watched as the serpent began to make its way back up the tree. *How does it know there are eggs in that nest?* she wondered. They seemed so safe way up there. That's when she started thinking about her own children. They seemed safe, out of Satan's reach, but were they?

Julie and Greg had three children. Their family was experiencing many of the normal growing pains associated with children entering their teenage years. She and Greg sometimes argued over how to discipline them, or not discipline them, as it seemed to be the case with Greg.

She prayed for their oldest, Rachel, age thirteen; Robert, age twelve; and for Gail, age four, their surprise child. Her prayer was simple: "Lord, protect my children from the Evil One. Lord, keep my children out of Satan's reach."

When she said "Amen," she looked up at the tree and noticed that the snake was getting closer to the nest of eggs. Nothing protected the mockingbirds' eggs from the advances of the serpent. Then she thought about the passage from Genesis. God didn't even protect Adam and Eve from the advances of the serpent. The serpent was free to roam the Garden. It occurred to her that she was asking God for the wrong thing. If God didn't keep Adam and Eve away from the advances of Satan why would God do that for her children? Not even Jesus was protected from Satan's advances.

The mockingbirds spotted the snake again. This time they attracted the attention of neighboring birds. Before long, there were eight to ten birds diving at the snake until its advancements were rebuffed. The snake finally turned away and headed back down the tree, no doubt until another opportune time, which is just how the Bible describes Satan after he failed to get Jesus to sin in the wilderness. "When the devil had finished all this tempting, he left him until an opportune time" (Luke 4:13).

Julie thought about the birds. Though two birds were enough to turn away the serpent the first time, it took a community of birds to turn around the serpent the second time. Julie felt convicted. She and Greg were good people. They believed in God. They loved their children. But they were wrong in thinking their efforts alone were enough to help their children turn away the temptations that would come their way. She knew her children needed a community of believers to help them. She knew she and Greg needed a community of believers to help them turn away temptation, too.

Julie prayed again. This time she prayed for forgiveness, and she prayed she would be able to make the kinds of changes she needed to make to set the kind of example she wanted her children to follow. She prayed she would be able to convince her husband to make the changes he needed to make. She knew getting him off the golf course on Sunday mornings would not be easy.

She also believed the events that took place in that cemetery were not coincidental. She prayed that God would work through other events to speak to her husband as He had spoken to her in the cemetery.

When Julie got up, she didn't have to walk very far before she found the grave of her great-great-grandfather, Sidney Perkins. When she found the grave she could see an epitaph inscribed on the old marble. She stooped down to rub the marble with a flat stone. After she had removed years of grime, the words became clear enough to read. "Sidney Perkins, 1825-1910. 'By faith he still speaks, even though he is dead.' Hebrews 11:4"

His faith still speaks. Those words bounced inside Julie's head. Then she began to recall a few of the stories about him that her grandfather had told her. She remembered that Sidney Perkins was instrumental in getting Mt. Sinai Primitive Baptist built in the late 1800's. She remembered the story about him and his wife, Maudie Bell, taking in three orphaned children, even though they already had eight mouths to feed. She remembered reading in the history of the church minutes that once when the church was without a pastor, Sidney Perkins filled the pulpit until one was called.

Then it hit her that her faith was in part due to this man's faith. She understood the significance of the Scripture from Hebrews 11:4. His faith had spoken to her even though he was dead. His faith had spoken to his children, who shared the faith with their children, who shared it with their children, who had shared the faith with her.

Julie felt convicted because she knew those words from Hebrews could not be placed on her tombstone or on her husband's. Although they were believers, she knew their faith wasn't speaking loudly enough for others to hear, much less if they died.

Julie paused at the gate and whispered one last prayer. "Lord, I need to make some changes. Help me begin to live my life in such a way that when I die, my faith will still speak. Help me live my life right now in such a way that my faith will speak to my children and help protect them from evil. Help my children to see a faith in me that they will want for themselves, a faith strong enough to rebuff the advances of Satan. Thank you for reminding me that even though Satan offers life, he peddles death. Amen."

Meanwhile, as she walked out of the gate of the cemetery, the serpent began making its way back up the tree.

WALKING THE LABYRINTH

1. Do you have a friend or family member whose life ended too soon? Has the person's death caused you to question God or the meaning of life?

2. Close your eyes. Imagine that you have died. How old are you? Who are your survivors? What does the minister say about you in the eulogy?

3. Take inventory of your life. Where is most of your emphasis placed, on that which is bound to this world or on that which can be laid up as treasure in heaven?

4. It's the year 2083. After an interment at the local cemetery, a person notices your grave. On the tombstone is your name, date of birth, date of death, and an epitaph. The epitaph catches the person by surprise and causes her to think about her own mortality and/or what is of the most value in life. What is the epitaph on your tombstone?

5. If you received word from your physician that you had an incurable disease which would take your life within a year, are there places you would go, things you would do,

relationships you would mend, things you would say, or areas of your life that would become either more or less important? Why not choose one or two of the things you have identified and make them a priority immediately? You may have only a short time to live and not know it.

6. In the story, "By Faith He Still Speaks, Even Though He Is Dead," the birds learned that together they could turn away the advances of the serpent. What temptations are you trying to rebuff on your own? Which ones do you need the support of friends to turn away? Are you forgetting that the church should be used as a community to help you turn away the advances of Satan?

7. For your life to speak by faith generations from now, how must you live your life differently or what must you continue to do in order for your faithful voice to still be heard?

CHAPTER FIVE

struggle is a part of the journey

A NEST AMONG THE THORNS

Jim felt proud that he had managed to swing a deal to buy a piece of property that once belonged to his great-grandfather. As he walked over the 100-acre field, he dreamed of building a house on a little knoll surrounded on three sides by a stand of oaks and pines. The field was mostly a maze of brier bushes and weeds. When his great-grandfather owned the land, he planted cotton as a cash crop and an assortment of row crops to feed his family.

In one corner of the field were a pile of boards and some old rusty sheets of tin. It was all that remained of a small barn once used to board the mules. From underneath one of the boards, Jim saw what looked like a handle to an old plow. He reached down and pulled it out. Indeed, it was one side of an old push plow. The rusty v-shaped end was still attached. He caressed the handle as if it were made of gold. He gripped the weathered handle, imagining how his great-grandfather must have gripped it a thousand times.

Jim looked at the small blade on the end of the handle, and then he lifted his eyes to see the brier-infested field that lay before him. He couldn't imagine turning all that soil with one of those plows, even if a strong mule pulled it.

He remembered stories his grandmother used to tell him about when she was a little girl, the youngest of thirteen children. Her mother had died giving birth to her so an older sister raised her. She remembered how her daddy struggled to earn enough money from his cotton crop to keep them clothed and fed and how difficult it was for him without a wife. Several of her brothers dropped out of school to help their father farm or to find a job that would help the family make ends meet. Life was difficult. A look across that open, brier-infested field was enough to convince him that his life had been relatively easy compared to his ancestors'.

Even so, if pressed in conversation, Jim would admit he was far from being happy and far from being free from troubles in spite of his talent for making money. There were plenty of brier bushes growing in his life, choking out his joy. The latest and most earth-shattering issue involved the pregnancy of his seventeen-year-old daughter. The father, or "boy" as Jim referred to him, was a class-mate of his daughter's. The encounter apparently occurred during an un-chaperoned party at one of their friends' home. Jim wanted to break the boy in two, but he knew that wouldn't solve anything. To make matters worse, the issue had caused a lot of friction between him and his wife. They were each blaming the other for a lack of attention and a lack of control of their daughter.

Jim had been used to plowing through whatever problems arose in his life, especially at work. He was a problem solver. His managerial skills were excellent. But at home his managerial skills didn't seem to help much.

As he sat on an old stump, he felt some solidarity with the brier-infested field. He realized that he had allowed his family life to go unattended while he climbed the corporate ladder. Though he knew that even the best of families experienced crises, he couldn't help but wonder if he were not partly to blame for his daughter's pregnancy. He hadn't been there for her or for his wife for several years. What would he do now? How would they get through this issue? He wondered if he should encourage his daughter to have an abortion. Wouldn't that be a logical solution? Wouldn't that be sort of like plowing under the thorns?

As he sat on the old stump pondering his next move, a bird flew into the brier thicket. The sudden fluttering of wings caught him off guard. Next he heard what sounded like the chirping of baby birds. Then the bird flew out of the thicket as quickly as it had come.

Jim got up and slowly made his way into the brier thicket, having to pull the briers from his jeans. They hurt as some of them found their way into his flesh. But he was determined to find the source of the chirping sounds. After several yards of careful steps, he found a small bird's nest among the thorns. The vibration of the thicket caused three birds to stick out their long necks. He could see their wide-open beaks as each bird hoped to be the recipient of the next meal.

As Jim drove home that day, he kept thinking about that bird, how it had made a nest among the thorns. After going to bed that night, he couldn't sleep. He lay awake thinking of his daughter and the thorny issues that lay ahead for her and the family.

The next day was Friday—Good Friday as it is sometimes called. Jim wasn't much of a churchgoer, but he had been invited by a friend to attend a Good Friday service at the local Episcopal Church. Jim wasn't Episcopalian, but he wasn't looking for a particular church; he was looking for answers.

His mind drifted during the hymns, the readings, and even the prayers. He was half-paying attention to the homily when the rector directed their attention to a banner that hung over the pulpit, depicting the crown of thorns Jesus wore as the soldiers mocked him as a king before executing him on a cross.

Then the rector said: "Thorns remind us that life is difficult and sometimes painful. The Book of Genesis tells us that Adam and Eve were cast out of the Garden of Eden because of their sin. Adam had to earn a living by the sweat of his brow as he battled the thorns and thistles for food. From that day on, the thorns served as a reminder of their sin."

Then the rector turned over to the New Testament and began speaking of how Christ took our sins upon himself on Good Friday, symbolized by the crown of thorns the soldiers placed upon his head. Then with passion in his voice, the rector read from John's Gospel: "The soldiers twisted together a crown of thorns and put it on his head. They clothed him in a purple robe and went up to him again and again, saying, 'Hail, king of the Jews!' And they struck him in the face" (John 19:2-3).

As he read, Jim's mind darted back to the field of thorns, to the sin in his own life, then to the picture Scripture drew of Jesus wearing a crown of thorns.

Then the rector said, "The blood that ran from Jesus' brow and the blood that ran as nails were driven into his hands and his feet was shed in order to cover the sins of humanity. When the blood of Jesus covers our sins, we are forgiven and new life is birthed within us. Then we can take flight, mounting up with wings as eagles, and rise to new heights. For some of you here today, life may look bleak, but hold on. God can show you how to make a nest among the thorns. That's what God did on Easter morning when Jesus was raised from the dead: He made a nest among the thorns."

Jim felt tears welling up in his eyes. It was as if God had him especially in mind for that message. How could the rector have known about his experience in the brier field, of seeing that nest, of needing to know how to guide his daughter? It didn't matter. What now mattered to Jim was what should have mattered all along—a commitment to extend the same love and grace to his daughter that he believed the Lord was extending to him.

As the church celebrated the Eucharist, Jim's inhibitions to go forward to receive communion were gone. He knelt at the altar and cupped his hands. The rector came by and placed a piece of bread in them. Then he came by with the cup. As Jim dipped the bread in the cup, he prayed that the Lord would forgive him of misplaced priorities, of neglecting his family, and for not taking time to worship. As he prayed, he felt light, as if a weight had been lifted from his shoulders.

As he left the church that day, Jim still had problems. The thorns had not disappeared. He had to go back into the world and face them. But he knew what he needed to do. Among the thorns there was new life that needed to be birthed in their family: physical life and spiritual life. He left the Episcopal Church that day with hope that Jesus could help his family build a nest among the thorns. He wasn't yet soaring as an eagle, but he felt his wings had begun to grow.

THE INEVITABILITY OF STRUGGLE

Many people like a challenge, but not very many people like to struggle, especially with issues that have the potential to pull us under like an ocean undertow. Yet, struggle can also produce muscle. The benefits a body builder gets from lifting weight come as a result of struggle. Therefore, struggle is neither positive nor negative. It is neutral. Whether it is positive or negative depends on what we do with it.

Humankind has engaged in struggle since the creation. Look closely at the story of Adam and Eve. In the second account of creation in Genesis 2, creation seems to have existed in perfect harmony. There doesn't seem to be any survival of the fittest among the animals and there is no struggle on the part of Adam and Eve to survive, either. Even so, in the midst of all that God had created and called good, evil was present, represented in the form of the serpent.

This story does not attempt to explain where evil came from or how the serpent was created. It just reports the presence of evil as fact. Because evil was present, struggle was birthed in the hearts and minds of Adam and Eve, who were tempted to disobey God.

It was inevitable for struggle to be a part of God's creation because Adam and Eve were made with the capacity to sin. Part of what it means to be human is to have the capacity to sin. God created humankind with free will. We have the opportunity to make good decisions and the capacity to make poor ones.

Struggle entered the world because of the possibility of sin. God did not protect Adam and Eve from the possibility of sin. Though it would be wrong to say God created evil, God created an environment where struggle was inevitable. As long as there is the possibility of sin, there will be struggle because as humans we must wrestle with many of the decisions we make. Here is a more positive view of struggle: whenever struggle exists, there is the potential to do the Lord's will.

I once read of an elderly couple who desired to employ a chauffeur. The lady of the house advertised; the applicants were screened, and four suitable candidates were brought before her for the final selection. She called the prospective chauffeurs to her balcony and pointed out a brick wall alongside the driveway. Then she asked the men, "How close do you think you could come to that wall without scratching my car?" The first man felt he could drive within a foot of the wall without damaging the car. The second felt sure he could come within six inches. The third believed he could get within three inches. The fourth candidate said, "I do not know how close I could come to the wall without damaging your car. Instead, I would try to stay as far away from that wall as I could." He got the job.

This is good advice that can be applied to areas of our lives where we are vulnerable to temptation, areas where we are likely to lose the struggle. We should stay as far away as possible from temptation. Had Eve not gotten so close to the tree of knowledge of good and evil, she would not have noticed that the tree was "good for food and pleasant to the eyes" (Genesis 3:6a). This is one way to minimize struggle. But human nature is to get closer and closer to the forbidden fruit, like a moth coming to a flame. Eventually, we get our wings clipped or worse, we crash and burn.

However, life cannot be lived in such a way that we escape all temptation. Not even Jesus escaped temptation. Not even Jesus escaped struggle. The same evil force that tempted Eve in the garden was present in the wilderness to tempt Jesus to base his ministry on a selfish agenda.

Jesus' struggle is nowhere more obvious than in the hours before being arrested by the Romans as he prayed in the Garden of Gethsemane for God to spare him the agony of the cross. His struggle was so intense that the Bible says that "being in anguish, he prayed more earnestly, and his sweat was like drops of blood falling to the ground" (Luke 22:43-44).

In the story, "A Nest among the Thorns," Jim was struggling to keep his family together. At first glance his daughter's decision to have sex with her boyfriend didn't appear to have anything to do with him. The choice was hers and hers alone. However, Jim couldn't deny that he'd been preoccupied with the desire to acquire his father's home place and with his steady rise within the corporation where he worked. Communication in the family was lacking, and the news of his daughter's pregnancy raised the height of struggle to an unprecedented level.

The patch of briers became a strong metaphor for Jim and his struggles. The metaphor blossomed as he sat in the Good Friday service and listened as the rector connected the briers which grew as a result of the fall of man to the story of the thorns Jesus wore on his head before and during his crucifixion.

Jim realized that he had created some of his own thorns with poor decisions he had made but that Jesus had taken them upon himself. "But he was pierced for our transgressions, he was crushed for our iniquities; the punishment that brought us peace was upon him, and by his wounds we are healed" (Isaiah 53:5).

The imagery of Jesus wearing a crown of thorns at his beating and crucifixion is powerful. Jesus saw the cross as an opportunity to take upon himself the sins of the world. However, Jesus did not come to remove us from all the trials of life. Part of the human experience is to struggle. That has been true ever since the fall of humankind.

Temptation continues to knock on every door. If we give in to temptation, our problems only deepen. If we win the battle against temptation our lives can escape the clutches of evil. Jesus proved that to be true as he overcame temptation. However, if we give in to temptation our struggle against evil only deepens.

We must constantly be attentive to the Holy Spirit who evaluates our lives, convicts us of sin, and empowers us to turn away from sin and embrace God's way of life. Understanding that no amount of effort is going to take away all our struggles in life is helpful because we can then turn our attention to building nests where new life is birthed in a world filled with thorns.

THE PRIVILEGE OF STRUGGLE

Jesus came to show us how to do battle with the evil of this world. Jesus came to show us how to struggle and emerge victorious. Blessed are those who see struggle as an opportunity to overcome evil, to lift up the name of Jesus, to make the right choice, not only so we can find our way, but so others can be influenced by us and in turn find their way. When looked at life from this perspective, struggle can be seen as an opportunity to advance the kingdom of God.

In the old wood-frame classroom, I prepared for a new day of class as a fifth grader. It was close to spring, but the mornings were still brisk while the afternoons were warm and pleasant.

During exploration of the woods near my home and school, I had found a cocoon, which I carried to class to show my friends. We all wondered what kind of winged creature it might contain. We eagerly awaited its rebirth into the world.

Day after day passed. The outside temperature began to get warmer. We could see the moth moving inside the cocoon like a baby kicking inside her mother's womb.

As fifth graders we didn't know what a cesarean section was, but we performed one on the cocoon to birth the moth into the world. We had waited long enough. Besides, we thought we were doing the moth a favor by helping it emerge from the cocoon from which it was struggling to break free.

As we cut through the cocoon, we were amazed that a moth with a wing-span of about six inches emerged. I had seen moths that large at football games swirling around the lights that lit the field. Never had I held one so large and beautiful.

After all the classmates had a chance to see the insect I helped birth into the world, it was time to let it fly. I gave the insect a little lift into the air, but it plummeted to the hardwood floor like a rock. It flapped its wings on the floor moving in half-circles. I picked up the moth to give it another opportunity to fly, but again it hit the floor with a thud. Though its wings looked healthy, we never did get the moth to fly. Many years later I read that it is during the struggle of emerging from the cocoon that the moth's wings are strengthened for flight. By keeping the moth from struggling, I had inadvertently kept it from flying.

Marcus Wells is a physical therapist in Moultrie, Georgia. In 2004 he traveled to Honduras with a medical mission team. While he was there, a woman brought in her eighteen-month-old son who could not walk or hold up his head while lying on his stomach. Not having experience in pediatric therapy, Marcus feared he would be unable to help the child. Then he remembered something he had learned in school. He took the child by the arms and gently lowered him until his feet came in contact with a cold surface. This angered the child, who started to cry. But it also jump-started the child's legs. He moved them up and down, trying to avoid the cold sensation. Then he stiffened his legs in anger, enough to support his weight briefly. Marcus told the mother she was going to have to make her child mad. Before this child would ever walk, he would first have to struggle. The mom needed to force the child to struggle.

Condoleezza Rice, President Bush's national security advisor and later secretary of state, is the daughter of a second-generation minister, the Reverend John W. Rice, Jr., who pastored Westminister Presbyterian Church in Birmingham, Alabama during the beginning of the civil rights era. Rice grew up in an environment of struggle, punctuated by that infamous day when a bomb exploded killing four young black girls, one of whom was Rice's classmate. She was only two blocks away in her father's church and felt the floor shake when the bomb exploded.

Rice does not believe struggle and sorrow should be license to give way to self-doubt, to self-pity, and to defeat. Rather, struggle is "an opportunity to find a renewed spirit and a renewed strength to carry on." How else but through struggles, she said, "are we to get to know the full measure of the Lord's capacity for intervention in our lives? If there are no burdens, how can we know that he can be there to lift them?"[9]

Showing that she has allowed the roots of her heritage to grow deep within her soul, she recalled the words of a Negro Spiritual in a sermon she preached to a Presbyterian congregation in

California. She said, "In the most horrendous of conditions, when it must have seemed that there was no way out, nowhere to go, slaves raised their voices in 'Nobody Knows the Trouble I've Seen. Glory. Hallelujah.' " Glory? Hallelujah? How can people sing "glory, hallelujah" about the troubles they've seen? Rice believes these words show the paradox of the human condition, the belief that struggle is actually a privilege.

The Apostle Paul is in agreement with Dr. Rice. In writing to the church in Corinth, the Apostle Paul lifted up the example of the Macedonian churches who saw their trials as opportunities rather than setbacks.

> Out of the most severe trial, their overflowing joy and their extreme poverty welled up in rich generosity. For I testify that they gave as much as they were able, and even beyond their ability. Entirely on their own, they urgently pleaded with us for the privilege of sharing in this service to the saints.
>
> —2 Corinthians 8:2-4

Whether you and I mount up with wings as eagles and soar to great heights or whether we fail to develop the strength to take wing will largely be determined by what we decide to do with struggle as we find our way. Another key to finding our way is to see struggle as a privilege and an opportunity to become stronger, more faithful followers of Christ.

OPPORTUNITIES WITHIN THE STRUGGLE

In Chinese, there are two ways to interpret the word "crisis." One way means "danger." The other way means "opportunity." It all depends on one's perspective.

When I read about the missionary journeys of the Apostle Paul, I am amazed at how he interpreted times of crisis as times of opportunity. He was once beaten, along with his friend Silas, after refusing to stop preaching the gospel. They were thrown into prison. No doubt in severe pain, they managed to sing hymns to God during the night. An earthquake shook the prison and the doors in the prison were opened. The jailer immediately saw this crisis as a moment of danger. Should the prisoners have escaped, he might have faced death. Distraught, he prepared to take his own life, but Paul saw the crisis as an opportunity.

He shouted,

> "Don't harm yourself! We are all here!" The jailer called for lights, rushed in and fell trembling before Paul and Silas. He then brought them out and asked, "Sirs, what must I do to be saved?" They replied, "Believe in the Lord Jesus, and you will be saved—you and your household." Then they spoke the word of the Lord to him and to all the others in his house. At that hour of the night the jailer took them and washed their wounds; then immediately he and all his family were baptized.
>
> —Acts 16:28-33

Paul received a public flogging on four other occasions, was stoned on another occasion, survived three shipwrecks, and once spent a night and a day in the open sea. He told the churches of Galatia that he had been in danger from rivers, bandits, his own countrymen, and Gentiles. He told them he knew what it was like to be hungry, thirsty, and cold. Yet, over and over, Paul viewed these crises as opportunities. Even when he was brought before Roman authorities like Felix and King Agrippa, Paul saw these as opportunities to share his experience of conversion, prompting King Agrippa to ask Paul, "Do you think that in such a short time you can persuade me to be Christian?" (Acts 26:28).

I admit, in the thick of the battle I often view a crisis as a moment of danger rather than a moment of opportunity. I do well when I am helping other people walk through their moments of crisis. When it's my crisis, it's different. I am still learning to place all situations in God's hands and understand that through it all, God will not leave me or forsake me. Therefore, my attitude should be different throughout difficult and trying times.

Paul wrote to the church at Thessalonica, "Be joyful always; pray continually; give thanks in all circumstances, for this is God's will for you in Christ Jesus" (1 Thessalonians 5:16-18).

Paul didn't say to be thankful for everything. But in all circumstances, we can find something to be thankful for. Approaching circumstances with this attitude can help us find opportunities in the midst of a crisis.

One day a farmer's donkey fell down into a well. The animal cried piteously for hours as the farmer tried to figure out what to do. Finally, he decided the animal was old, and the well needed to be covered up anyway; it just wasn't worth it to retrieve the donkey. He invited all his neighbors to come over and help him. They all grabbed a shovel and began to shovel dirt into the well.

At first, the donkey realized what was happening and cried horribly. Then, to everyone's amazement he quieted down. A few shovel loads later, the farmer finally looked down the well. He was astonished at what he saw. With each shovel of dirt that hit the donkey's back, it was doing something amazing. He would shake it off and take a step up. As the farmer's neighbors continued to shovel dirt on top of the animal, he would shake it off and take a step up. Pretty soon, everyone was amazed as the donkey stepped up over the edge of the well and happily trotted off!

Rarely does a week go by that life doesn't shovel dirt or something a little smellier on us. When we are at our lowest point, we are the most vulnerable to the attacks of evil. Though we may feel powerless over our circumstances, circumstances cannot dictate the attitude we have or the resolve we have to carry on. Such decisions are made within each individual. When trouble and hard times come, we can resign ourselves to defeat and be covered up in our trouble, or we can shake off the dirt and take a step up.

When we hear a story about the donkey that shook off the dirt and took a step up, we know we are dealing with a tall tale, but the message it carries is no tall tale at all. It's a message of hope, a message of perseverance, a message which reminds us that when life gives us lemons, we still can choose to turn them into lemonade.

Paul and Silas took a terrible flogging because of their witness of Jesus. Instead of shutting up, they used their sufferings as a platform to lift up Jesus. God had changed the hearts of these men to the point where they were not filled with bitterness for their captors but with love. Their voices could not be silenced because joy is not a matter of circumstances: it is a matter of the heart.

Robert R. Updegraff says that we need to learn to be thankful for troubles we experience on our job. He makes the point that if jobs were easy, anybody could do them. We earn our money because we have to deal with difficult people and difficult situations. Otherwise, someone else would be given our job for half of what we are being paid. Updegraff challenges us to handle troubles cheerfully and with good judgment. If we view them as opportunities rather than irritations, he says we will find ourselves getting ahead at a surprising rate.[10]

That's what was beginning to happen for Jim in the story, "A Nest among the Thorns." Jim began to see his daughter's mistake as an opportunity to extend to her the grace and love she needed. He realized that although the situation was fraught with challenges, there was also the opportunity for spiritual life to be birthed along with the physical. Jim began to see how a nest of goodness, warmth, love, and compassion could be built among the thorns. It wasn't an ideal situation, but it was an opportunity. Recognizing that can make the difference between finding and losing our way.

STRUGGLING WITH TEENAGE BOUNDARIES

Through twenty-one years of marriage, Jim and Kate had learned how to communicate, to solve problems, and to compromise. Marriage, they learned, is a give-and-take relationship, and it is always better if both try to give more than they take. They found this to be especially true after their children came along.

When the children hit the teenage years, Jim and Kate realized that just as in the first years of their marriage, they seemed more on edge with each other. They were spending less and less time together. Their life, it seemed, revolved around their three teenage boys. Though they enjoyed being parents, they discovered that the teenage years were different from the other years, a lot different.

One issue they struggled with was knowing where to set the boundaries for their boys. Mark, 17, Daniel, 16, and Hunter, 13, were each very different. Their different personalities, plus their different ages, meant the boundaries the couple set for them were different and in constant flux.

It's natural that teenagers want to break free from their parents' boundaries and test their limits. It was with Jim and Kate's oldest son, Mark, that the battle over boundaries was most intense.

Getting ready to enter his senior year in high school, Mark began to question a lot of his parents' rules. Their discussions usually ended with his father saying with great frustration, "End of discussion! As long as you are under our roof you'll live by our rules! We don't have to explain the reason for every decision we make!" This ended the discussion but usually widened the gap of understanding between them. Both usually went their separate ways to let the steam boil away.

After such an exchange, Jim often retreated to his workshop and worked late building furniture. He often took Bullet with him. One thing Jim and his son had always had in common was their love for Bullet. They had brought Bullet home as a puppy the day Mark began first grade. He was Mark's dog, but Jim loved him just as much as his son did.

As Jim worked, he looked at Bullet lying contentedly on his pad. He wished raising kids were as easy as raising a dog. Most dogs and kids start out the same way: they both think the man of the house is perfect and both are usually the first ones to greet him at the end of the day. Jim chuckled to himself as he thought about that. Mark had known for several years that his dad wasn't perfect and had long stopped looking and running out to the truck to greet him on his return from work. But Bullet still jumped up and down and wagged his tail when he heard Jim's pickup coming down the driveway. *Dogs can be more forgiving than people,* Jim thought to himself.

Jim ran the last board through his saw and cut out the shop lights. Then he put ol' Bullet in the chain-linked fence for the night. Several times they tried letting him stay out, thinking he'd stay close by, but each time Bullet ran the neighborhood. The next morning he'd have a neighbor's boot or mop dragged up in the yard. The last time they didn't shut him up for the night, Bullet was hit by a car. After a hefty vet bill and a lot of worry, Bullet healed. Everyone agreed that the fence served a good purpose.

As Jim closed the gate, it occurred to him that they put Bullet in the fenced-in area each night because they loved him. He had room to move around, plenty actually. He had freedom but it was within the boundaries they chose for him.

The next morning at breakfast, Jim figured Mark would pick up the conversation from the night before about driving the truck to the beach for the weekend with some friends. He usually didn't give up after one try. But Jim didn't let Mark get started before he put a little bit of his country wisdom to work.

"Mark, I've decided that I'm not going to put Bullet behind that fence any more at night. In fact, I don't like that fence at all. I'm going to tear it down this weekend, and I want you to help me."

Mark protested immediately, "But Dad, you know what happens whenever Bullet's left out. He's likely to get hurt again. Besides, you know that Mr. Watkins told us he'd shoot him if he ever caught him digging again in his yard."

"No, Mark. I've decided that Bullet is old enough that he doesn't need any boundaries. How old is he now, anyway? Eleven? Now, let's see. In dog years that's about…"

"Dad, that's not funny. I thought you cared for Bullet more than that. We keep him behind that fence because we love him. I don't want anything to happen to him. If you tear down the fence, I'll let him sleep in my room."

"I'm glad you see it that way, Mark," Jim said. "Last night when I put him up, it occurred to me that he was the reason we put up that fence several years ago. He's got boundaries because they are good for him. We set boundaries for him because we love him."

About that time Mark began to see the spark in his dad's eye. He knew this conversation was headed somewhere. He knew he'd been set up.

"Mark, about our conversation last night—I want to remind you that your mother and I set boundaries for you because we love you. Now we admit, your boundaries are changing. The older you get and the more you prove to us you are responsible and can be trusted with the space we give you, the more space you'll get. We know that you don't like boundaries at all. But if we didn't love you, we wouldn't set any. Think about it: if we set boundaries for our dog because we love him, how much more important is it that we set boundaries for you because we love you? Soon you will leave home and go to college. But as long as you are in our home, we will set boundaries for you because we love you. At college, we won't be there to set boundaries for you. You will be setting your own, I hope. We hope and pray that because you have had to live within boundaries in our home, you will have the discipline to set boundaries and live within them when you leave us."

It was over. Mark had withstood another lecture marathon. But he did begin to see his dad's point. He didn't like admitting when his dad had a good point.

Surprisingly, he gave his dad some assurance, in his own teenage way, that he understood the point. "Dad, don't worry about me. When I go off to college I won't be like Bullet and run crazy at night."

They both smiled as they finished their biscuits. Jim felt good about the conversation. Maybe he had gotten through to Mark. He wasn't sure. It's hard to tell with teenagers. Only with the passing of time do parents usually know for sure. But Jim remembered a biblical proverb that was becoming more and more important to him as his boys got older: "Train a child in the way he should go, and when he is old he will not turn from it" (Proverbs 22:6).

After finishing his last swallow of milk, Mark tried one more time. "Dad, are you sure you won't change your mind about this weekend?"

There was a brief silence which gave Mark momentary hope. "No, Mark," his dad said. "I'm going to keep this boundary up a little longer. Soon you'll be old enough to make that trip and many more, but not now."

Mark knew his dad wouldn't change his mind. Though he really wanted to make that trip, deep down he was glad his dad had kept that boundary up a little longer. Strangely, he felt some security in his dad's "not now." But more than security, he felt loved.

WALKING THE LABYRINTH

1. What struggles are you currently facing? List the ways you have tried to overcome your struggles. Why have they failed? Brainstorm new ways of overcoming your struggles. Ask God to lead you to find a new way to work through your current struggles.

2. Some struggles are caused by our own sin. Are you facing struggles caused by your sin? Read the following passages of Scripture: Psalm 103:12; Luke 11:4; John 20:23; 1 John 1:9. What do these passages tell you about forgiveness?

3. Some struggles are caused by the sin of others which can lead to conflict or to broken fellowship. If you sat down and had a conversation with Jesus, how would Jesus tell you to respond to those who have sinned against you?

4. Other struggles are due to no sin of anyone in particular but are just part of living in a world filled with briers that threaten to choke out our joy. When we cannot remove the briers, we need to learn to make a nest among them.

Are there any briers that threaten your joy that you cannot remove? How might you make a nest among the briers and make the best of a difficult situation?

5. Do you ever give God thanks for allowing you to struggle? How might the opportunity to struggle be contributing to strengthening your faith?

6. There is no magic wand to wave to take away our struggles. However, nothing puts our struggles in perspective like entering God's sanctuary and worshiping with a community of believers. Recommit yourself today to regular participation with a Bible-believing, Spirit-filled church. Read Psalm 73. What struggles did the Psalmist have? What did worship have to do with resolving his struggles?

7. Spend some time reflecting on how boundaries have changed for you through your life and how you responded to those who set boundaries for you. Did you rebel against those who set boundaries for you? Did you comply? Do you still rebel? Comply? If you are now the one who is setting boundaries for others, what are you learning about yourself? Do you hate setting boundaries for others? Does it come easy because you understand that boundaries are an expression of love?

8. Think about it: if we set boundaries for our dog because we love him, how much more important is it that we set boundaries for children because we love them?

9. If you are a parent who has problems setting boundaries or if you have a teenager who has a problem accepting boundaries, conflict is the end result. Rebellion is around the corner. Do yourself a favor. Schedule a family counseling session. Find your way through your issues together. Don't point fingers at one another. Don't blame. Just acknowledge that you have problems you can't solve on your own. Find a qualified counselor who can help you find your way through your family struggles. It's not defeat to seek help. It's defeat to be in denial and fall apart.

CHAPTER SIX

finding our way takes some courage

Several years ago a couple from Texas attended an evening service at Trinity Baptist Church. Afterwards the couple introduced themselves. Mr. and Mrs. Mel Henderson, a couple from Arlington, Texas, were back in Moultrie, Georgia retracing some of their footsteps made during the early years of their marriage.

Mel Henderson had come to Moultrie to receive pilot training at Spence Field. During that time, he and his wife joined Trinity Baptist Church. As with many of those who trained to be pilots, their time in Moultrie was brief, but significant.

Mel Henderson made many friends during his time in Moultrie. One of those friends was Jack Tomes. After their training Mel and Jack went separate ways, only to be reunited decades later at military reunions. At one of those reunions, Jack shared the following story with Mel. Mel brought this story back home to Moultrie and shared it with me. I've entitled the story, "Jack, Will You Sing Again?"

This riveting story reminds us that finding our way sometimes takes great courage. Jack's courage demonstrates that when we have found something worth dying or suffering for, we have found something worth living for, or in this case Someone worth living for, Jesus our Lord.

JACK, WILL YOU SING AGAIN?

"Jack, will you sing again?" his comrades asked. A year had passed since Jack last used his baritone voice to pierce the gloom of the prison, the infamous "Hanoi Hilton." This Vietnamese prison held as many as 268 Americans during the Vietnam War. Some of them, like Jack Tomes, were downed fighter pilots, a trophy for the Vietnamese.

In the 1950's, Moultrie, Georgia was home to many young men who came to begin their flying career with the U.S. Air Force. Jack Tomes was one of these men, earning his wings as a part of Class 56-V. He later left Moultrie. He went on to further his training and became a fighter pilot.

Not only were his pilot skills honed in Moultrie, but he also found a place to use his crisp baritone voice. Ever on the lookout for talent, Miss Neta Belle Scarborough once gave him the lead solo when the Trinity Baptist Church choir presented "The Seven Last Words of Christ."

On his last mission over the jungles of Vietnam, Jack was shot down and became a POW. He was interned at The Hanoi Hilton, notorious for its brutal treatment of American prisoners. Any violation of the rules received swift punishment. One Christmas Eve, Jack ignored the rules because he could not ignore his desire to sing of the God who was with him. To everyone's surprise, a baritone voice broke the silence of the night as Jack sang, "Silent night, holy night; all is calm, all is bright..."

The guards, startled to hear such a deliberate violation, were a little slow to react, and Jack finished singing just as they burst into his cell. Then the punishment began. It was very severe. Jack thought he would die from his beating. Recovery was slow and prolonged.

Days turned into weeks, weeks into months, and the months added another year that Jack and others spent in the torture facility. As Christmas approached again, someone asked the question, "Jack, will you sing again?" Jack said he wasn't sure. His body reminded him of the price he had paid the year before. He might not survive another beating.

Once again, he stood in his cell and looked out at the sky, twinkling stars filling his view and the power of Christ filling his heart. God gave him the courage to sing again. As the year before, the baritone voice pierced the silence. Though he sang "Silent Night," the night became filled with the sound of Christmas. The Viet Cong had taken away his freedom, but they could not take away his joy or his song.

Before the guards had time to inflict another beating on him, an amazing thing happened. Someone in another cell began to sing with Jack, then another, and another until Jack was singing with a choir once again. Jack's courage was contagious. His spirit was infectious. The camp guards were caught unprepared and began to consider what should be done. With so many to punish, they chose to do nothing. The guards did not come for Jack that night. In fact, the camp rules were later changed to allow the prisoners of the camp to sing a Christmas hymn on Christmas Eve.

Jesus once said, "And do not fear those who kill the body but cannot kill the soul. But rather fear Him who is able to destroy both soul and body in hell" (Matthew 10:28-29 NKJV).

Not only had Jack found his way. Jack found the courage to announce to fellow prison mates and to his enemy guards that he did not fear the guards or what they could do to him. Jack feared the Lord. Through his rich baritone voice, Jack courageously announced that Jesus is the way, the truth, and the life. The Viet Cong managed to lock up his body, but his spirit they could not touch.

Courage and Freedom Are Birthed in Our Hearts

The story of Jack Tomes reminds me of the scene in the movie, *Shawshank Redemption*, starring Tim Robbins, Clancy Brown, and Morgan Freeman. In the movie, Andy Dufresne, an intelligent man wrongly convicted of killing his wife, is found to be useful by the prisoners, the guards, and even the warden for doing their tax returns.

In addition to mailing their tax returns, Andy writes and mails letter after letter to the State Senate asking for funds to begin a prison library. To the shock and surprise of Andy and the staff at Shawshank Prison, a check from the State Senate of $200 arrives one day along with boxes filled with books donated by the Library District.

Agitated that Andy's request has actually been answered after six years of sending letters, Byron Hadley, captain of the guard, orders him to clear all the boxes out of the office before the warden returns. As he opens boxes like a starving man looking for food, to his surprise he finds a gray and green phonograph player with the words "Portland Public School District" stenciled on the side. In addition, he finds some used record albums. He flips through the music. There are some classic Nat King Coles and some Bing Crosbys. Then he comes across Mozart's "Le Nozze de Figaro." He pulls the record from the stack, slips it from its sleeve and places it on the phonograph. The needle makes a scratching sound until it finds the groove. The song is "Deuttino: Che soave zeffiretto," a duet sung by Susanna and the Contessa.

Andy barricades the front door, turns on the P.A. microphone, and then courageously flicks the toggle button on the microphone. Suddenly the music is broadcast all over Shawshank prison. Andy leans back in the chair, props his feet on the desk, puts his hands behind his head and soaks up every note, every word, defiantly ignoring repeated calls from guards to turn the music off.

The prisoners all stop their work. Whether they are in the plate shop, the laundry room, the wood shop, or out in prison yard, they all stop and gaze at the speakers. The hearts of killers and robbers and rapists are suddenly touched by words that sound as if they were delivered by angels.

Here are the words of Andy's friend, Red, used to describe what that music was like to the ears of men starving for something other than the demanding tones of guardsmen shouting out their orders:

I have no idea to this day what them two Italian ladies were singin' about. Truth is, I don't want to know. Some things are best left unsaid. I like to think they were singin' about something so beautiful it can't be expressed in words, and makes your heart ache because of it. I tell you, those voices soared. Higher and farther than anybody in a gray place dares to dream. It was like some beautiful bird flapped into our drab little cage and made these walls dissolve away…and for the briefest of moments—every last man at Shawshank felt free.[11]

We live in a binding world. We are fettered with guilt, loneliness, sin, grief, addictions, poor health, ignorance, persecution, poverty, financial woes, just to name a few. We often need help from others to escape from these and other maladies. We are fools if we think we have the strength to break out of bondage on our own. However, there comes a time, a moment of opportunity, where we must decide to exercise enough courage to step out and meet the Lord.

The Psalmist said: "Wait on the LORD; Be of good courage, And He shall strengthen your heart; Wait, I say, on the LORD" (Psalm 27:14 NKJV).

Here, courage is not something we find within us that we have created on our own. This kind of courage comes from our trust in the Lord. It is this kind of courage that Moses had as he went before Pharaoh to demand the release of the Hebrew people. It is this kind of courage that helped David slay the giant, Goliath. It is this kind of courage Elijah had as he challenged the prophets to Baal on Mount Carmel. It is this kind of courage that Stephen had as he gave witness before his accusers who stoned him to death once he gave witness to the Lord. It is this kind of courage that Paul and Silas had as they sang hymns in prison after they had been beaten for proclaiming the word of God.

This kind of courage comes as a result of spending time with the Lord. By waiting on the Lord, we will be given the courage we need to find our way when the way becomes difficult.

Courage to Find Our Way is Gained from Others

A few years ago I was enjoying some beach time at Panama City Beach, Florida, when I noticed a v-shaped flock of pelicans high up in the sky. I thought about the benefits the birds enjoyed through their cooperation and their organized flight. The lead bird, the first one to cut through the air, expends more energy than the others. Those behind the lead bird form a v-shape pattern which creates lift so the birds in the back don't have to work as hard as those in front.

Flying in such an organized pattern demonstrates shared leadership because they are constantly rotating positions. Eventually the lead bird works to the back and the birds in the back eventually work to the front. They share equally in the flight, each benefiting from the work of the other.

In the midst of this group of v-shaped flying pelicans, I noticed something really strange. There was one oddball in the group. A duck was flying among the pelican formation. It amused me. My mind flashed back to a jingle I remember from "Sesame Street": "One of these things is not like the others/ One of these things just doesn't belong/ Can you tell which thing is not like the others/ By the time I finish my song?" That duck certainly wasn't like the others. It didn't seem to belong there.

As I watched that flight of pelicans and that duck, I saw something else that surprised me. The duck participated in the rotation of the flight pattern. Eventually, the pelicans allowed the duck to take the lead. They treated him as an equal. For a few moments, the duck was leading a group of pelicans, putting forth the most effort so those behind him could benefit from his labor. I bet the duck felt the added work was an honor, just as it was an honor to benefit from the draft created by the others when he flew in the back of the formation.

One of the great temptations of life is always to group with those of like feather. There are understandable reasons for this, but when those reasons have a basis in sinful prejudice, regardless of whether that prejudice is based on economics, race, nationality, religion, or gender, we must seek forgiveness and repent. We are also tempted to exclude others from our group because of similar reasons, and we must look to God to forgive us when we yield to this temptation as well. There are times I have had to repent of both of these sins.

It takes courage to step out and work with those different from us. It takes courage to let go of our stereotypes and seek to know others on a personal level. It takes courage to admit our sins of prejudice and allow God to help us build a relationship with those different from us. It takes courage to go through Samaria instead of walking around it. It takes courage to dream that the world can be a different place, a better place.

Martin Luther King, Jr. saw something of God's kingdom when he dreamed of a day when his children would live where they would not be judged by the color of their skin but by the content of their character; a day when "little black boys and black girls will be able to join hands with little white boys and little white girls as sisters and brothers."[12] If we are going to find our way, we must realize that as long as ducks fly in their formation and pelicans fly in theirs, we cannot reach the heights or fly the distances laid out for us by our Creator.

We've come a long way, but we still have a long way to go. How shall we continue to get the ducks and the pelicans and the sea gulls and the eagles and the sparrows all flying together in the same formation, working toward a common goal, sharing in both the leadership and the benefits of the leadership of others? The answer comes to me in another children's song, this one from Sunday School: "Red and yellow, black and white/ They are precious in his sight/ Jesus loves the little children of the world." This simple children's song reminds us that this is what God's formation looks like. It's up to us to make it a reality.

In order to make such dreams a reality, we must learn how to fly in God's formation. We must maintain strong discipline. When we don't, our decisions not only affect us but others flying in the formation with us.

We must remember that if we are living as God commands, if we are seeking to do the Lord's will, we will feel a lift from his Spirit. At times we may not feel we belong in God's formation because of our own shortcomings, especially in a leadership role, but that's not for us to decide. God does the calling. We are supposed to hear His call and with courage obediently fall in formation.

A key to finding our way is to travel with fellow Christians, both learning from them and sharing with them along the way. As we flap our spiritual wings, we will get stronger and stronger. Eventually we will be asked to lead in a way that's in keeping with the spiritual gift(s) given to us by the Lord.

> Praise and glory to the One who gives strength to the weary and increases the power of the weak. Even youths grow tired and weary, and young men stumble and fall; but those who hope in the LORD will renew their strength. They will soar on wings like eagles; they will run and not grow weary, they will walk and not be faint."
>
> —Isaiah 41:29

It Takes Courage to Sing in the Rain

Perhaps the most memorable dance number on film was performed by Gene Kelly and Debbie Reynolds in the 1952 film, *Singing in the Rain*. The characters they played were so beset with romance that they ignored their surroundings. They danced in spite of the rain, swinging from lampposts, splashing in rain puddles. The rain did not dampen their mood. They were filled with joy and happiness in the midst of clouds and rain.

The Book of Acts tells of Paul and Silas being arrested. They were arrested in the city of Philippi for preaching the gospel. After being beaten, they were thrown into prison. Even so, "at midnight Paul and Silas were praying and singing hymns to God" (Acts 16:25). They were bruised. They were cut. They were bleeding. They were in pain. The circumstances were far from pleasant. Yet in their hearts, Paul and Silas were rejoicing. Hymns bubbled from their hearts and flowed to their lips as they sang during the night. They were singing in the rain.

Dr. Viktor Frankl, author of *Man's Search for Meaning,* was imprisoned by the Nazis in the Second World War because he was a Jew. His wife, children, and parents were all killed in the Holocaust. The Gestapo made him strip. He stood there totally naked. As they cut away his wedding band, Viktor said to himself, "You can take away my wife, you can take away my children, you can strip me of my clothes and my freedom, but there is one thing no person can ever take away from me—and that is my freedom to choose how I will react to what happens to me!"[13]

I'm not suggesting that terrible circumstances shouldn't cause us to grieve, to be angry, or to be afraid. God created us with these emotions. They bubble up whether we want them to or not. But God also created us with minds and hearts that have the ability to raise us above circumstances and point people to the power of a Holy God.

Luke, the writer of Acts, says that when Paul and Silas were singing, "the other prisoners were listening to them." Imagine the reaction they must have had. There's no doubt they listened in disbelief that after what had happened to Paul and Silas, they could still have an attitude of joy.

When adversity, change, and hardships come our way, people are naturally curious how we will respond. Will our words be bitter or will our words reflect the spirit of Christ? Will we have the courage to continue to praise God or will we curse God instead? People will be listening for our response.

One of the more amazing things about this story in Acts is how soon after being flogged and thrown into prison were Paul and Silas singing and influencing others.

It doesn't take long to influence others. People quickly notice what kind of Spirit we have. When adversity comes, it is an opportunity to demonstrate God's power and guidance in our lives. It's an opportunity to influence others for Christ. How we handle adversity is a sign of our true identity. Our real colors fly during times of adversity.

George Stewart wrote:

> Weak men are the slaves of what happens. Strong men are masters
> of what happens. Weak men are victims of their environment.
> Strong men are victors in any environment. Strong men may
> not change the circumstances, but they will use them, compel
> them to serve, and bend them to their purposes. They may not
> be able to change the direction of the wind, but somehow they
> will coerce the wind to fill their sails while they drive the tiller
> over to keep their course.[14]

Paul and Silas epitomized Stewart's words. Their songs oozed
out of their spirits because their hearts were full of doxology and
love even after the men were arrested, flogged, and thrown into
prison. They could sing in the rain because the Lord Jesus reigned
in their hearts. The power given them from the Lord helped them
to rise above their situation.

The story in Acts says their singing was interrupted by an
earthquake. This seemed like bad news on top of bad news. The
ground shook, releasing the fetters that held the prisoners in their
cells. Surprisingly, no one tried to escape. Why? Because they were
influenced by Paul and Silas. The prisoners were willing to follow
the lead of a couple of men they had just met. Had they escaped on
the jailer's watch, he likely would have been put to death, which
is why he drew his sword to kill himself but was stopped by Paul
and Silas.

The jailer was consumed with his problems, while Paul and
Silas demonstrated the courage to rise above theirs with the help
of the Lord. It is human nature to become consumed in our problems. It takes the Spirit of the living God to enable us to sing in
the rain; to help someone else overcome problems when we are
chained to our own.

The jailer, seeing their faith, their courage, and their unbeliev-
able concern for him, asked what he must do to be saved.

> They replied, "Believe in the Lord Jesus, and you will be
> saved—you and your household." Then they spoke the word of
> the Lord to him and to all the others in his house. At that hour

of the night the jailer took them and washed their wounds; then immediately he and all his family were baptized. The jailer brought them into his house and set a meal before them; he was filled with joy because he had come to believe in God—he and his whole family.

—Acts 16:31-34

We sometimes have no choice about the adversity we have to face, but we are always left with a choice of how we will respond. The way we respond could make the difference in whether we find our way and whether we convince others that Jesus is the key to finding our way. But first, we ourselves must believe that He is.

Jack Tomes believed it. In the Hanoi Hilton he had the freedom to sing in the rain, to swing from lampposts and splash in puddles. No doubt he suffered greatly with the rest of the POW's, but he demonstrated that his joy wasn't contingent upon his circumstances but upon the love and strength of God.

Walking the Labyrinth

1. What word would others use to describe your faith in God? Jack Tomes' faith was infectious. In what way is your faith infectious?

2. Sometimes brief escapes from life's binding fetters are all we can manage. Don't underestimate the importance of brief escapes. How might you help others escape briefly from the fetters of their lives?

3. Have you witnessed or have you demonstrated courageous moments in your life? Ask God for the courage to stand up for him at all times and in all situations. Better yet, think of a specific situation in your life where you need more courage and ask God to give you the power you need to stand firm in your faith.

4. Circumstances sometimes bring joy, but joy is not contingent upon circumstances. Have you witnessed the life of those who had every reason to be bitter but exuded a joyful spirit instead? When you walk out of this labyrinth today, may God grant you the resolve to respond to life's lemons

by making lemonade. Remember, you have the freedom to choose how you will react to that which life throws your way.

5. Think of some people whose lives have been an inspiration to yours. What made their lives especially noteworthy to you? People are watching you. Someone, somewhere is taking his or her cue from your life. Where are you leading this person?

6. Whenever we fly in formation with a body of believers, there is an uplifting of spirit which we cannot get by any other means. If you are benefiting from such a fellowship with other believers, give God thanks and ask God to help you use your gift(s) for the benefit of your fellowship of believers. If you have strayed from regular participation in the body of believers, meditate on Hebrews 10:25: "Let us not give up meeting together, as some are in the habit of doing, but let us encourage one another—and all the more as you see the Day approaching."

CHAPTER SEVEN

Learning from god's world along the way

Illustration by Tina Piemonte

GROW WHERE YOU ARE PLANTED

Henry A. Corn was born early one spring in the top of a massive oak tree, the largest of the forest. Through the spring and into the summer, Henry grew and began to dream of fall. Fall was the topic of conversation among all of Henry's siblings. All had been taught that they were valuable to Mother Earth and would make their own unique contributions. Some would become food for squirrels. Others would decay and become part of the soil. Still others would find fertile ground and grow into a tree. Only one or two would ever become as large or massive as the Great Mother Tree. So when the wind blew and the branches swayed, the acorns shared their dreams with one another.

When the green of the leaves began to disappear, and one by one they began to let go of the tree, the acorns knew their time was near to take the great fall to the earth below. Henry A. Corn remembered the words of the Mother Tree. She had told him that each acorn was important and had purpose. Henry believed her, but he was not content to be squirrel food or rot for the sake of the earth. Henry set his sights higher. He wanted to be that one acorn which grew to become a mighty oak, mightier even than the Great Mother Tree herself.

Henry could feel his crown beginning to loosen from the twig that fastened him to the branch. He looked below and picked out a fertile spot to land. Time for the fall was near. He hoped he could free himself at the break of day and roll to his designated spot.

As night fell, a huge storm rolled into the forest, and the limbs of the Mother Tree swayed violently. Henry was shaken loose from her grip and was thrown through the air, far from his designated landing.

When the light from the east streaked through the forest floor the next morning, Henry discovered his plight was worse than he imagined. Instead of landing on fertile soil, he rested on top of a boulder, wedged in a crack. How unfortunate! He could see the fertile ground in the distance where he had hoped to land. He had missed his only opportunity. Henry felt sorry for himself. He could see that other acorns had landed in fertile soil, and he envied them. He even envied those that landed in the nearby stream. At least they had mobility and some chance to find soil downstream.

He looked at the Great Mother Tree. He longed to be like her. What could he do? He called out to her for advice. The songbirds brought him her message. "Honor the Creator. Grow where you are planted," they chirped. It was a beautiful melody, but it was not the song he wanted to hear. The melody and its message played over and over in his mind through the remaining fall and into the winter. He nestled down in the crack. The wind blew bits of soil onto the rock and into the crack which eventually covered him. He felt entombed and a bit depressed. Then spring arrived. The weather warmed. The winds blew warm again. Henry A. Corn knew that he had a choice. He could die, or he could grow where he was planted.

With much effort Henry A. Corn sent a shoot into the limited soil below him. It was painful but rewarding. Within a few days, up through the soil emerged a green shoot that soon became a young sapling. Henry D. Tree had emerged. The branches of the Great Mother Tree bowed low in affirmation. Henry was growing where he was planted. The Creator of the forest was pleased and sent sun and rain to assist his growth. Through the spring Henry grew. His growth was stunted because of the limited amount of soil. Yet, he grew with great hope and promise of becoming all he could be.

As time passed, people who traveled the forest trail were first drawn to massive Mother Tree. But as they turned toward the stream, Henry was the tree that became their inspiration. He was uplifted by all as an example of determination, faith, and hope. Though he reached only five feet in total height, Henry stood tall. He never became a mighty oak, but he grew where he was planted. His decision pleased the Creator and made the Great Mother Tree proud.

Perhaps most important of all was the contribution Henry made to the forest. The acorns he produced, though few in number, were stronger and more resilient than those of the Mother Tree. Through the years, the squirrels and birds carried them to other places in the forest that needed new trees. More than any other tree in the forest, the acorns from Henry D. Tree produced many oaks that rivaled the size and strength of the Great Mother Tree. The forest was a better place because one little acorn blown off his course decided to grow where he was planted.

LEARNING FROM NATURE

Nature is a wonderful teacher. The salmon teaches determination as she finds her way upstream for hundreds of miles to find the place to lay her eggs before she dies. The butterfly teaches all who feel like a wretched worm that transformation is possible. The spider teaches that ingenuity and hard work can put food on the table.

As the clouds open and close, we are reminded that we are not self-sufficient. The need for rain causes us to look heavenward and remember that the very basic elements of life cannot be created by man but are gifts of God.

Nature has as many lessons to teach as ever. However, we are as far removed from nature as we have ever been. Closed up in our homes, we no longer hear the chipmunk chirp and watch it scurry around at the break of day for food. With its erratic, nervous movements, the insecure chipmunk teaches that one must be on guard for danger. Instinctively, the animal knows that when the red-tail hawk launches itself from its perch and swoops down with power and accuracy upon its prey, few will escape its powerful talons. The hawk teaches that confidence and power can be coupled with grace and beauty.

The ocean waves beat against the shore without ceasing, a low tide, then a high tide, low, then high. Its rhythm is calculated by the gravitational pull of the moon, an invisible force that constrains the beach to make its sands a welcome mat for the salty waters. When is the last time you sat and watched the waves and pondered the invisible forces that keep your life in rhythm?

From the soil, life springs forth. Bulbs that have lain dormant through the winter will soon produce an array of color: tulips, hyacinths, lilies, and daffodils. The azalea bushes and the dogwood trees will have their place in the sun as well. They will splash their color among other foliage, dazzling us with their beauty. These plants teach us not to discount that which seems to be without beauty. Sometimes beauty is hidden. It is not absent, only dormant. Under the right conditions it will blossom forth.

Jesus paid attention to nature and sometimes used nature to teach about the Kingdom of God. Once he said:

> Look at the birds of the air; they do not sow or reap or store away in barns, and yet your heavenly Father feeds them. Are you not much more valuable than they? Who of you by worrying can add a single hour to his life? And why do you worry about clothes? See how the lilies of the field grow. They do not labor or spin. Yet I tell you that not even Solomon in all his splendor was dressed like one of these. If that is how God clothes the grass of the field, which is here today and tomorrow is thrown into the fire, will he not much more clothe you, O you of little faith? So do not worry, saying, "What shall we eat?" or "What shall we drink?" or "What shall we wear?" For the pagans run after all these things, and your heavenly Father knows that you need them. But seek first his kingdom and his righteousness, and all these things will be given to you as well. Therefore do not worry about tomorrow, for tomorrow will worry about itself. Each day has enough trouble of its own.
>
> —Matthew 6:26-34

Get out of the house. Turn off the TV. Get out in the yard and the woods. Take a walk by a stream. Put your hands in the soil. Observe nature, God's creation. God was there in the beginning. God is still there now, waiting to teach us if we are willing to watch and observe.

CAUGHT IN THE CREVICE OF THE ROCK

The story of Henry A. Corn came to me while I was on a trip to Dick's Creek in Northeast Georgia with a group of boys and their fathers. I became amused by the determination of a tree that was growing in the crevice of the rock.

At times we end up in places where we planned to land. Planning and goal setting are keys to finding our way, but life doesn't allow us to write our own script; some of it, yes, but never all of it. We end up in crevices we never dreamed about, expected, or desired. When we end up in those places, we have to decide whether we will grow in spite of our circumstances or whether we will grow bitter because of our circumstances.

Many biblical personalities demonstrate the kind of character God wants us to develop when we find ourselves in the crevices of life. Consider Joseph, the favorite son of Jacob (Israel).

> Now Israel loved Joseph more than all his children, because he was the son of his old age. Also he made him a tunic of many colors. But when his brothers saw that their father loved him more than all his brothers, they hated him and could not speak peaceably to him. Now Joseph had a dream, and he told it to his brothers; and they hated him even more. So he said to them, "Please hear this dream which I have dreamed: There we were, binding sheaves in the field. Then behold, my sheaf arose and also stood upright; and indeed your sheaves stood all around and bowed down to my sheaf." And his brothers said to him, "Shall you indeed reign over us? Or shall you indeed have dominion over us?" So they hated him even more for his dreams and for his words.
>
> —Genesis 37:3-8 NKJV

These brothers plotted to kill Joseph but when a company of Ishmaelites came through from Gilead with their camels, bearing spices, balm, and myrrh, on their way down to Egypt, the brothers sold Joseph to them as a slave. What a deep crevice! This certainly wasn't the way Joseph thought his life would go.

He was bought by Potiphar, an officer of Pharaoh, captain of the guard who put Joseph in charge of his household. Because of his high morals, Joseph refused the advances of Potiphar's wife, who then lied to the guards, declaring he had tried to rape her. Joseph was thrown into prison. Could his crevice have been any deeper?

While there he rightly interpreted the dreams of Pharaoh's chief butler and chief baker, both of whom had been thrown into prison by Pharaoh. To the butler he said his dream meant in three days he would be restored to his position. To the baker he said his dream meant in three days he would be dead. Both happened as Joseph predicted.

Some time later Pharaoh had a dream that none of his magicians or wise men understood. The butler remembered Joseph had been able to rightly discern his dream and the dream of the baker, and he shared this information with Pharaoh. Joseph was summoned by Pharaoh, who told him his dream. Joseph told Pharaoh the dream meant there would be seven years of bountiful harvest followed by seven years of severe famine. Joseph explained that God had brought this to his attention so he could adequately prepare for the famine. He advised Pharaoh to find a man to set up an organized system of collecting the abundant grain in the years ahead to prepare for the famine. Pharaoh chose Joseph.

> Pharaoh said to Joseph, "Inasmuch as God has shown you all this, there is no one as discerning and wise as you. You shall be over my house, and all my people shall be ruled according to your word; only in regard to the throne will I be greater than you." And Pharaoh said to Joseph, "See, I have set you over all the land of Egypt."
>
> —Genesis 41:39-41

Joseph grew where he was planted. He looked for his place in an environment that he did not choose. He looked for God to use him where he was even though it wasn't where he wanted to be.

Life carries us to places not of our choosing. It would be easy to lose perspective and to feel that since life has dealt us such a bad hand we must not be fulfilling the purpose we were called to fulfill.

Some believe everything happens for a reason. These people are looking for oversimplified answers to complex issues of life that often have no logical explanation. Bad things have always happened to good people and always will. Trying to affix a reason for every bad thing that happens to us in life is counterproductive. Usually, it's only when we see events in the rear view mirror of life that we can come to any conclusions. Such was the case of Joseph, who was shocked to see his brothers show up years later in Egypt. They were sent there by their father Jacob to find food because of the famine.

In that dramatic and tearful scene where Joseph reveals to his brothers his true identity, Joseph said to them,

> "Do not be afraid, for am I in the place of God? But as for you, you meant evil against me; but God meant it for good, in order to bring it about as it is this day, to save many people alive. Now therefore, do not be afraid; I will provide for you and your little ones." And he comforted them and spoke kindly to them.
> —Genesis 50:19-21 NKJV

God does not put us in every crevice in which we become lodged. However, once we are in a crevice, God is ready to assist us. Sometimes God helps us out and sometimes God helps us grow where we are planted. At times we may be able to move out of a situation that is less than ideal and grow from the experience. At other times this is not possible. When we are stuck in the crevice, questions about our purpose in life may surface. Before we can grow, we may need to back up and settle some of life's deeper questions.

BACKING UP TO GO FORWARD

Peniel Baptist Church sits just inside the Dale County line from Barbour County, the county where my roots run deep. My great-grandfather, Reverend Fletcher Shirah, pastored Peniel Baptist for a total of twenty-eight years. He was called as pastor of the church on five different occasions. Many of those years the church was considered a "quarter-time" church, meaning it held services only one Sunday a month. Because of this commonality in the early 1900's, Reverend Shirah usually held more than one pastorate at a time.

Peniel Baptist sits on top of a hill. It's steep enough to make you winded if you tried to run up the hill. Apparently, it was steep enough to be a challenge for the 1934 Ford that Reverend Shirah used to drive to church.

I met a man recently who attended Peniel as a boy. He remembered that Reverend Shirah's Ford had a bad clutch. The car would get halfway up the hill but no farther. The boy and his father would walk down the hill and help Reverend Shirah turn his car around. "The car had a good reverse," the man said. "He'd back his car the rest of the way up the hill. He backed that car all over this country."

There's a good lesson here: sometimes we have to back up to go forward. A mathematician knows this well. It's the reason she uses a pencil with an eraser rather than an ink pen. Ever tried to use a pencil and follow a maze from one end to the other? Sometimes you hit a dead end, and you have to back up and find another path. How many times have people had to do that with a career that hit a dead end? Many people have backed up to get more training or earned another degree in order to go forward.

Consider an athlete who sustains a major injury. To go forward he may have surgery and go through rehabilitation. A stroke victim often has to relearn to walk or even talk. Both of these have to back up to go forward.

When watching NASCAR, occasionally I see a driver overshoot his pit stop. Those cars aren't designed to go in reverse. They only have forward speeds. The pit crew runs to the driver's aid and rolls the car back into the pits.

Many people don't believe in backing up. They only have forward speeds. Forward speeds help us reach many goals, but, in some situations, forward speeds don't help. Sometimes we must back up to go forward.

When we wrong others, wound others, and damage relationships, they do not move forward unless we back up and make amends with those we have wounded.

The words, "I'm sorry. I was wrong. Will you forgive me?" are not in everyone's vocabulary. Some people only know how to go forward. These people reach a point where no more progress can be made. The relationship stalls. Bitter roots take hold.

Not every hill in life can be climbed alone. Sometimes we need a push, some encouragement, some direction, and some advice, especially when we have wounded people and damaged our relationships with them. Sometimes we need a trusted friend to remind us that we need to swallow our pride, back up, and seek forgiveness. Sometimes we need to be that trusted friend for others.

Before Jesus ascended into heaven, he sat down on the beach with Peter, who had abandoned Jesus during the crucifixion and denied he knew Jesus three times. The resurrected Jesus met Peter where he first met him, by the lake. There Jesus made sure Peter understood he had been forgiven. He gave Peter the charge of feeding his sheep, a metaphor for leading people into the Kingdom.

Before Peter could be the rock Jesus predicted he would one day be, Jesus knew Peter needed to back up and attend to old issues. Sometimes life dictates that we need to back up before we can go forward.

FEELING SMALL

Henry A. Corn had to come to terms with the fact that he'd never be a mighty oak tree like his mother. The circumstances didn't allow him to grow large, but that didn't mean he could not grow with significance.

A key to helping us find our way is to understand that every person is significant. The contributions we each make will not be weighed by God on a comparative scale but rather in accordance with what each of us has been given. God expects us to use what we've been given, whatever it is, in whatever proportions, for His glory.

I've always been small. I was the smallest kid in my grade, from first through the twelfth. Even now, sopping wet, I weigh about 140 pounds. My father tells me I was pulled before I was ripe. Although I'm small in stature, I usually feel that I have something to contribute, but that wasn't true during some of my adolescent years. Even so, I'm prone to occasional moments of feeling that my contributions in life are too small, which discourages and depresses me.

Several years ago I traveled to British Columbia for a week of Bible study, worship, and sermon preparation with a group of ministers from various denominations. The week away from all the demands and responsibilities of life was uplifting and refreshing.

As I sat on the plane for the return flight home, I enjoyed the beauty of the snow-capped mountains, ice-covered lakes, seagoing vessels, and slow movements of what I knew to be a fast-paced world. Against such a backdrop, I felt small. Compared to the vastness of God's world, to the knowledge of other people in this world, to my ability or lack thereof to solve the problems which this world faces, I felt small. Most of all, compared to the God of heaven and earth, my smallness overwhelmed me.

Being gone for a week away from family, church, and community reminded me that life moves on with or without me. The family still functioned, the church didn't fold, and the community didn't miss me. That thought pattern became depressing.

The psalmist once commented about his feeling of smallness. "When I consider your heavens, the work of your fingers, the moon and the stars, which you have set in place, what is man that you are mindful of him, the son of man that you care for him?" (Psalm 8:3-4).

Then it occurred to me. Feeling small or being small is not the same as being insignificant. A bee is small, but think of the flowers that would not mature without its help. A tear is small, but without it how would we be able to cleanse our souls of grief and sadness? A hug is small, but without one how would we feel the depth and the warmth of another person's love?

As I reflected on these metaphors, I remembered the motto of the First Baptist Church in Hartwell, Georgia during the years Dr. Hugh Kirby served as her pastor: "Doing small things so great things can happen."

Jesus was born in a small, insignificant town just outside Jerusalem. He grew up in a small, insignificant village called Nazareth. Other than the time his parents carried him to Egypt as a baby, he never traveled more than a few hundred miles away from either of those two places. He spent most of his time of ministry working with a small group of twelve men. He showed them through his

133

actions that no person was too small or too insignificant for the love of God.

Jesus taught them that the kingdom of God is like a grain of mustard seed, the least of all the seeds. Yet, when it is planted, it becomes the greatest of the herbs, growing like a tree, large enough for the birds to come and lodge in its branches. The mustard seed is small but not insignificant.

You and I are small. Compared to the vastness of God's world, we are small but we are not insignificant. The same psalmist that pondered his smallness in God's created order was reminded that God made us a little lower than the angels and crowned us with glory and honor. (Psalm 8:5) God gave us dominion over the works of his hands. That doesn't sound insignificant, does it?

Henry A. Corn grew where he was planted. Though disappointed that his stature didn't measure up to the Mother Tree, he realized his contribution to the forest was no less significant, nor was the inspiration he instilled in others who recognized how he had grown despite obstacles incurred.

If you feel small, that's not so bad. In fact, it is rather humbling, and at times we need to be humbled. We must remember that feeling small does not mean we are insignificant. What you contribute to this world today may be small, but it will not be insignificant. It's the small acts of us all that God uses to save this world from being swallowed up in darkness. Think of yourself as a light that needs to shine. In the midst of darkness, one small burning candle can make all the difference. Don't put your candle under a bucket. Light it and let it shine. God will take your small light and make great things happen. Believe it. One small light is all it takes to help us find our way.

WALKING THE LABYRINTH

1. As we seek to find our way, the winds of life will sometimes blow us off course. We may not end up where we wanted to be. Sometimes, the best we can do is to grow where we are planted. Are you growing where you are currently planted? If not, what might you do to begin putting down some spiritual roots where you are?

2. Missed opportunities can leave us depressed. A person's perspective often dictates whether growth can still come out of a lost opportunity. What opportunities have you missed? What lessons have you learned from missed opportunities? Be an optimist. Learn from missed opportunities and be ready when the next one comes along.

3. Most of us are little fish in a big world. The world would keep right on moving even if we were not here. It would be easy to feel insignificant in such a world but don't believe it. Your life is significant! God's responsible for placing you here. God doesn't deal with trivial issues. You have purpose. Part of your purpose is to glorify your Creator with your

life. Like a seed, we must "die to self in order to grow in Christ." Meditate on John 12:24-26.

4. Make a commitment to spend more time in nature, God's cathedral. Go for a walk. If possible, find somewhere to sit down. Be still and use all five senses to become aware of God's environment. Contemplate your place in God's vast world.

5. Honor your Creator. Grow where you are planted. Are there risks in such advice? Is there a price to pay? By following such advice, do we limit our potential or do we help guarantee success?

endnotes

1. SwanShadow, "What are you, Peanuts?" SwanShadow Thinks Out Loud, http://www.swanshadow.com/2005/04/what-are-you-peanuts.html (accessed June 2, 2005).

2. Otis Redding, "Sittin' on the Dock of the Bay Lyrics," Lyrics-Depot, http://www.lyricsdepot.com/otis-redding%25sitting-on-the-dock-of-the-bay.html (accessed May 22, 2005).

3. Billy Graham, "Which Way to Heaven?" Jokes Related to Christianity, http://www.broadcaster.org.uk/section2/jokes/christianjokes.html (accessed May 22, 2005).

4. United Feature Syndicate, Inc. "Peanuts," July 7, 1989.

5. Charles Laurence, "George Bush's Comrades Eaten by Their Japanese POW Guards," JamesBradley.com-Press. http://www.http://www.jamesbradley.com/press/sunday_fp.htm (accessed June 2, 2005).

6. Anton Chaitkin & Tarpley G. Webster, George Bush: The Unauthorized Biography, Chapter 6, "Bush in World War II." http://www.tarpley.net/bush6.htm.

7. William E. Thorn, Catch the Little Foxes That Spoil the Vine, (New York: Fleming H. Revell, 1980).

8. Tim McGraw. "Live Like You Were Dying." Sing365. Com, http://www.sing365.com/music/lyric.nsf/Live-Like-

You-Were-Dying-lyrics-Tim-McGraw (accessed May 22, 2005).

9. Sheryl Henderson Blunt. "The Privilege of Struggle." *Christianity Today*, September, 2003, www.christianitytoday.com/ct/2003/009/33.44.html (accessed August 10, 2005)

10. Robert R. Updegraff. "Thankful for Troubles on the Job." *The Autoillustrator* 7.0 1988-1998. PEJan88.

11. Stephen King, The Shawshank Redemption. Wikiquote. http://en.wikiquote.org/wiki/The_Shawshank_Redemption (accessed May 22, 2005)

12. Martin Luther King, Jr., "I Have a Dream," Martin Luther King, Jr. I Have a Dream. http://www.google.com/search?hl=en&q=+%22little+black+boys+and+black+girls+will+be+able+to+join+hands+with+little+white+boys+and+little+white+girls+as+sisters+and+brothers.%22+&btnG=Google+Search (accessed May 23, 2005)

13. James S. Hewett, Illustrations Unlimited (Wheaton: Tyndale House Publishers, Inc., 1988) 278-279.

14. George C. Stewart, "Quotations that Focus on Perseverance." Great Expectations. http://www.greatexpectationsok.org/implementation_viewquotes.php?type=2 (accessed May 23, 2005)

To order additional copies of

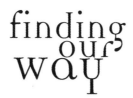

Send $16.50 per book to
Dr. Michael Helms,
Attn: Finding Our Way,
201 Twelfth Ave. SE, Moultrie, Georgia 31768.

Make checks payable to Canopy Road Horizons, LLC.
Price includes shipping.
Credit card orders can be placed by calling

1-877-421-READ (7323)

or by visiting our web site at
www.winepressbooks.com

Click on "Online Bookstore"
and enter in the search box the title of the book
"Finding Our Way"
or
the name of the author
"John Michael Helms"

and follow the instructions for purchasing the book.